12.35

D0870795

ALEXANDER ALEKHINE

(cr. 1927–1931)

The Steeplechase

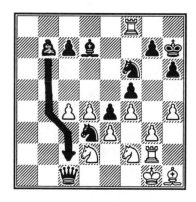

The Tactician's Handbook

Vol. 5

Pickard & Son
PUBLISHERS

Printed in the United States of America
ISBN: 1-886846-15-4
Cover by Ellis Graphics

This work is a revised and expanded translation of the Russian book "The Steeplechase," published by the author in 1999.

The
Steeplechase

Author: Victor Charushin
Editor: Sid Pickard
Translator: V.Charushin & A.Sychev

First Printing of English Edition: December 1999

Inquiries should be addressed to:

Pickard & Son, Publishers
P.O. Box 2320
Wylie, TX 75098
Tel (972) 429-9052
Fax (972) 429-9053
E-mail: chess@ChessCentral.com

Table of Contents

Table of Contents

Symbols

± White has a slight advantage   ∓ Black has a slight advantage

± White stands clearly better   ∓ Black stands clearly better

+− White is winning   −+ Black is winning

= the game is even   # checkmate

∞ the position is unclear   ⸗∞ with compensation

! an excellent move   !! a brilliant move

? a mistake   ?? a blunder

!? a move deserving attention   ?! a dubious move

△ with the idea   ⌓ better is

Introduction

"The pawn is the soul of chess" F.A.D. Philidor

As the soldier dreams of becoming a general, so the pawn desires to become a Queen.

In the opening stage of chess, pawns define the redoubtable structures of Black and White fortifications. In the middlegame, pawns serve as rams for crashing through the opponent's defenses, or as armored shields to beat off an attack. In the endgame, pawns are the masters who hold the game's fate in their hands.

In this 5th volume of *The Tactician's Handbook* we will investigate the combinative potential of pawns, with emphasis on opening and middlegame play.

Let's look, for example, at the White d2-pawn. On its initial square this pawn carries out only defensive functions, but with each move its offensive strength increases. On the fourth rank it provides a solid foothold in the center, but the pawn's advance to the fifth rank already constitutes an invasion into the opponent's territory, accompanied by definite threats. Its appearance on the sixth rank brings perturbation in the opponent's camp. Here a blockade is almost impossible, and any push to the seventh rank is very close to victory. Forward again to the eighth rank with transformation into a Queen – rather a rare thing in the middlegame – is a complete apotheosis!

The pawn's road forward is not studded with roses: it must overcome numerous obstacles created by the opponent. Thus the march turns into a Steeplechase – a race through obstacles.

Of course, the name only represents artistically the combination's main point and must not be understood literally. Here the "chase" is a pawn charge or breakthrough (with intermediate moves), and the "barriers" are opposing units that directly, or indirectly, influence the "racer's" route.

The following position illustrates these points.

(see next diagram)

The d4-pawn is at the starting gate. The initial advance is directly influenced by the enemy e5-pawn, so the first move breaks down this barrier.

Game 1
Charushin, V
1998

White to play and win

1.de5! ♚e7 **2.ef6** (In the same
manner the f6-pawn is eliminated)
2...♚e8 (Now the Black King
controls f7, and seems to stop any
further charge of the noisome pawn.
However...) **3.f7!!** (The finish! This
pawn forces itself to the seventh rank
despite all. The decision follows
shortly) **3...♚e7 4.♖d8 ♚d8** (The
spiteful 4...♚f7 only prolongs the
suffering) **5.f8=♛ +−**

As it happened, to reach the eighth
rank an intermediate move was
needed. Starting from the fourth
rank, therefore, the pawn required
three moves to reach the seventh
rank, and five moves to gain the
eighth. These steps will be seen
repeatedly in the following pages!

Part One

Excelsior

The shades of night were falling fast,
As through an Alpine village passed
A youth, who bore, 'mid snow and ice,
A banner with the strange device,
Excelsior!
H.Longfellow, *"Excelsior"*

The most complex and spectacular kind of Steeplechase is the pawn's march from its initial position to the eighth rank, where its promotion takes place. This variety of Steeplechase we call "Excelsior."

To illustrate this theme, nothing serves better than the following well-known game, which the first Russian world champion considered to be the best of his chess career. Except where noted, the comments are those of Alekhine.

Game 2
Bogoljubow,E—Alekhine,A
Hastings 1922

1.d4 f5 (A risky defense, which up to the present I have adopted only very infrequently in serious games. But in the present game I had to play positively for a win in order to make sure of first prize, whereas a draw was sufficient for my opponent to secure third prize. Hence I found myself forced to run some risks which were, after all, justified by my result) **2.c4 ♘f6 3.g3** (It is better to prepare this flank development of the light-squared Bishop in the Dutch Defense before playing c2-c4, because now Black can advantageously exchange his dark-squared Bishop which has only a very limited range of action in this opening) **3...e6 4.♗g2** (This immediate fianchetto development, evolved by Steinitz and adopted later by Rubinstein, does not appear to be the best line of attack; Black with the succeeding move obtains at least equality) **4...♗b4 5.♗d2 ♗d2 6.♘d2** (The recapture 6.♕d2, followed by 7.♘c3, is a little better) **6...♘c6 7.♘gf3 0-0 8.0-0 d6 9.♕b3** (This maneuver does not prevent Black from realizing his plan, but at this point it is difficult to suggest a satisfactory line to play for White) **9...♔h8 10.♕c3 e5** (This advance is feasible, because after the exchanges in the center the Queen's Knight is attacked by the Black Queen) **11.e3** (If 11.de5 de5 12♘e5? ♘e5 13.♕e5, White's Knight would be *en prise* to Black's Queen) **11...a5!** (It was very important to prevent b2-b4 temporarily, as will be seen later) **12.b3** (Not

12.a3?! on account of 12...a4) **12...♛e8 13.a3 ♛h5** (Now Black has secured an attacking position, for White cannot answer 14.de5 de5 15.♞e5?? ♞e5 16.♛e5 on account of 16...♞g4, winning outright; nor could he play 14.b4? e4 15.♞e1 ab4 and wins) **14.h4** (A good defensive move, which secures new squares for his f3 Knight and revives the threat 15.de5) **14...♞g4 15.♞g5** (White seeks to dislodge Black's Knight at once by 16.f3, which, however, weakens his pawn position still further. Possibly 15.b4 would now be preferable) **15...♝d7 16.f3** (If 16.♝c6 ♝c6 17.f3, then 17...ed4! 18.fg4 dc3 19.gh5 cd2 [Steeplechase! V.Ch.] leads to the better endgame for Black) **16...♞f6 17.f4** (Already compulsory, in view of the threatened 17...f4!) **17...e4 18.♜fd1** (In order to protect the g-pawn [which was threatened by 18...♛g4 and 19...♞h5] by ♞f1. However, the preliminary advance 18.d5!, preventing Black from forming a center, would have yielded White more chances of a successful defense) **18...h6 19.♞h3 d5** (By this move Black completely wrecks his opponent's hopes in the center, and shortly seizes the initiative on the Queenside in a quite unexpected fashion) **20.♞f1 ♞e7** (Prepares 21...a4!) **21.a4 ♞c6** (Now the Knight can penetrate right into the hostile camp via b4 and d3) **22.♜d2**

♞b4 **23.♝h1** (The fact that White had to conjure up this complicated maneuver in order to create faint chances on the Kingside shows clearly the inferiority of his position) **23...♛e8** (This very strong move yields Black a new advantage in every case: either control of the d5-square after 24.cd5, or opening of a file on the Queenside after 24.c5 b5!, or lastly, as in the actual game, the win of a pawn) **24.♜g2** (White is still trying for 25.g4, but even this weak counter-chance will not be vouchsafed him) **24...dc4 25.bc4 ♝a4 26.♞f2 ♝d7 27.♞d2** (In this position there sounds the command, "On your marks! Get set! Go!" as the b7-pawn rushes forward. V.Ch.)

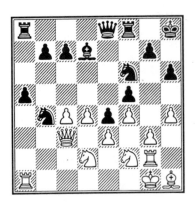

27...b5! (The renewal of the struggle for the center squares, a struggle whose vicissitudes will culminate in a stirring and original finish) **28.♞d1** (The Black b-pawn has passed the first two ranks without problems, but now there appears an original obstacle – one of its own pieces blocks the way. It will have to go! V.Ch.) **28...♞d3** (Preparing the ensuing combination. Instead, 28...bc4 would have been weak, for White's Knight would later have secured a good square at e5) **29.♖a5** (In the event of 29.cb5 ♝b5 30.♖a5 ♞d5 31.♕a3 ♖a5 32.♕a5 ♕c6, and Black launches a winning attack) **29...b4! 30.♖a8** (If 30.♕a1 ♖a5 31.♕a5, then after 31...♕a8! 32.♕a8 ♖a8, and Black's Rook penetrates into White's game with decisive effect) **30...bc3!** (As will be seen, this continuation is much stronger than 30...♕a8 31.♕b3 ♝a4 32.♕b1, after which White could still defend himself) **31.♖e8 c2!!** (The point! White cannot prevent this pawn from Queening) **32.♖f8 ♔h7 33.♞f2** (Clearly the only possible move) **33...c1=♕**

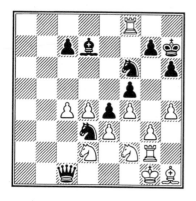

(The finish line! Having overcome all obstacles, the pawn nearly by force advanced along the route b7-b5-b4-c3-c2-c1. That's what "Excelsior" looks like, as performed by the world champion. Because of this combination, Black has a strategically won position. V.Ch.) **34.♞f1 ♞e1** (Threatening an unexpected and original "smothered mate") **35.♖h2 ♕c4** (Creating a threat of mate in a few moves, starting with 36...♝b5, which compels White to sacrifice the Exchange) **36.♖b8 ♝b5 37.♖b5 ♕b5 38.g4** (The only chance for White to prolong his resistance, but Black retorts with a fresh surprise move) **38...♞f3 39.♝f3 ef3 40.gf5** (Forced, for if 40.g5 Black would have obtained two united passed pawns after 40...♞g4 41.♞g4 fg4) **40...♕e2!!** (This move leads to a problematic position, in which White is unable to move any piece without exposing himself to immediate loss, for example, 41.♞h3 ♞g4!; 41.♞g4 ♞g4; or 41.♖h3 ♞e4 and wins. Hence, after two unimportant moves, he must play e3-e4, which leads to immediate liquidation with a won endgame for Black) **41.d5 ♔g8** (Not, however, the pausible move 41...h5, upon which White could have saved himself by 42.♞h3, followed by 43.♞g5) **42.h5 ♔h7 43.e4 ♞e4 44.♞e4 ♕e4 45.d6** (Being unable to defend his pawns, White endeavors to dislocate those of his opponenet, but his game is hopelessly lost) **45...cd6 46.f6 gf6 47.♖d2 ♕e2** (A pretty finish, worthy of this fine game. Black forces a winning pawn endgame) **48.♖e2 fe2 49.♔f2 ef1=♕ 50.♔f1 ♔g7 51.♔f2 ♔f7 52.♔e3 ♔e6 53.♔e4 d5, 0-1** (A.Alekhine)

The game makes a singularly bright impression, so much so that the combination might have been called "Alekhine's Passage"!

Across the Centuries

The history of the Steeplechase combination spans nearly 400 years. After Giulio Polero in the period 1585-1590 finally formulated the modern rules of chess play, there appeared an opportunity to demonstrate the full strenght of this tactical method. The next game was played at Duke Dacomo Buoncomanio's palace.

Game 3

Polerio,G—N.N.

Italy cr.1572-1584

1.e4 e5 2.f4 ef4 3.♘f3 g5 4.♗c4 ♗g7 5.h4 h6 6.d4 d6 7.♘c3 c6 8.hg5 hg5 9.♖h8 ♗h8 10.♘e5 de5 11.♕h5 ♕f6

(see next diagram)

12.de5! (Beginning a forced charge to the f7-square. The Queen at f6, an indirect obstacle, has to be overcome) **12...♕g7 13.e6** (No obstacle here!) **13...♘f6 14.ef7** (White's aim is achieved through a Steeplechase along the route d4-e5-e6-f7, overcoming two obstacles) **14...♔f8** (The game is cited by Gioachino Greco [Calabrese] in his treatise, where he points out variations such as 14...♔e7 15.♕e2 ♗e6 16.♗e6 ♔e6 17.♕c4 ♔e7 18.♕b4 ♔f7 19.♕b7 ♘bd7 20.♕a8 +– , and 14...♔d8 15.♕g5 ♕g5 16.f8=♕ ♔d7 17.♕h8 ♕g2 18.♕f6 f3 19.♕f7 ♔d6 20.♗f4 ♔c5 21.♘a4 ♔b4 [21...♔d4 22.c3 ♔e4 23.♘c5#] 22.♗d2 ♔a4 23.b3 ♔a3 24.♕e7 ♔b2 25.♕e5 ♔a3 [25...♔c2 26.♕c3#] 26.♗c1 ♔b4 27.c3#. After the text move, matters end more quickly!) **15.♗f4 ♘h5 16.♗d6#, 1-0**

Now we must leap forward 230 years! The deposed emperor of France, being imprisoned on a distant island, occupies his leisure dictating his memoirs and...playing chess.

Game 4
Napoleon I—General Bertrand
St. Helena 1818

1.♘f3 ♘c6 2.e4 e5 3.d4 ♘d4 4.♘d4 ed4 5.♗c4 ♗c5 6.c3 ♕e7 7.0-0 ♕e5 8.f4! (Interesting intentions. White invites the opponent's d4-pawn to start a Steeplechase. While it is busy overcoming obstacles, the emperor gets development for his pieces, consolidates the position, and achieves a winning game) **8...dc3 9.♔h1 cb2** (Black loses his Queen but immediately gets a new one) **10.♗f7** (An important intermediate move. The Bishop cannot be taken, for if 10...♔f7?, then 11.fe5 ♔e7 12.♗b2 follows) **10...♔d8 11.fe5 ba1=♕** (As a result, White for some time will play without a Rook, but the opponent's camp is ruined and victory is close at hand!)

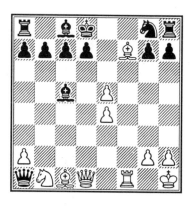

12.♗g8 ♗e7 (12...♖g8 13.♕d5 ♖f8 14.♖f8 ♗f8 15.♕f7 c6 [15...♕e5 16.♗g5!] 16.♕f8 ♔c7 17.♕d6 +−) **13.♕b3 a5 14.♖f8!** (A brilliant attacking finish!) **14...♗f8 15.♗g5 ♗e7 16.♗e7 ♔e7 17.♕f7 ♔d8 18.♕f8#, 1-0**

The fantastic potential of pawns on the march recalls a game by the "chess comet" Reno Charousek, a combinational genius.

Game 5
Charousek,R—Grunn
Hungary 1890

1.e4 e5 2.♘c3 ♘c6 3.f4 ef4 4.d4 ♕h4 5.♔e2 (The Steinitz Gambit) **5...d5 6.ed5** (Admirable. The race begins on the 6th move! Here is an obvious case of the Steeplechase and its efficiency in the opening) **6...♗g4 7.♘f3** (A compelled intermediate move) **7...0-0-0 8.dc6** (Two moves, two obstacles. Next is the third, the b7-pawn) **8...♗c5 9.cb7 ♔b8** (It's the end of the e4-d5-c6-b7 Steeplechase, and the beginning of material gains)

(see next diagram)

10.♘b5?! (White could have decided the game immmediately by 10.♕e1 ♕h5 11.♔d2 ♗f3 12.gf3 ♗d4 13.♗d3 ♕f3 14.♕f1 ♕g4 15.♘e2 +−) **10...a6 11.c3 ab5**

After 9...♔b8

12.♕b3 ♖e8 13.♔d3 ♗f3 14.gf3 ♕e1 15.♔c2 ♗b6 16.♕b5 ♘f6 17.♕a6 ♗a7 18.♗f4! ♕a1 19.♗c7! ♔c7 20.♕a7 ♖b8 21.♗b5! (A series of brilliant strokes in Chaousek's style!) **21...♕h1 22.♕c5 ♔b7 23.♕c6 ♔a7 24.♕a6#, 1-0**

In the next game a future Grandmaster was examined by the world champion, in a "seance" of simultaneous play.

Game 6
Rethy,P—Lasker,Em
Moravia 1910

1.e4 e5 2.♘f3 ♘c6 3.d4 ed4 4.♗c4 ♘f6 5.0-0 ♘e4 6.♖e1 d5 7.♗d5 ♕d5 8.♘c3 ♕d8 9.♘e4 ♗e6 10.c3?! (In the hope of 10...♗c4 11.♘f6. The usual continuations 10.♗g5 or 10.♘eg5 are better. Now there follows a Steeplechase along the route d4-c3-b2-a1!)

10...dc3! (As in the previous example, the combination is carried out in the opening. Of course, if 10...♗c4?? then 11.♘f6#) **11.♕b3 ♗b4** (An important intermediate move, x-raying the e1-square) **12.♘eg5 cb2! 13.♘e6 ba1=♕!** (The triumphant finish!) **14.♘d8 ♗e1 15.♘c6 ♕c1, 0-1.** White resigned because after 16.♗f7 ♔f8 there are no checks from a3 or b3.

During a Christmas tournament at Hastings, the victim of our combination was an ex-world champion, the chess machine J.R.Capablanca.

Game 7
Lilienthal,A—Capablanca,J
Hastings 1934

1.d4 ♘f6 2.c4 e6 3.♘c3 ♗b4 4.a3 ♗c3 5.bc3 b6 6.f3 d5 7.♗g5 h6 8.♗h4 ♗a6 9.e4 ♗c4 10.♗c4 dc4 11.♕a4 ♕d7 12.♕c4 ♕c6 13.♕d3 ♘bd7 14.♘e2 ♖d8 15.0-0 a5 16.♕c2 ♕c4 17.f4 (No, the start is not yet!

Another soldier will run the Steeple-chase) **17...♖c8 18.f5! e5**

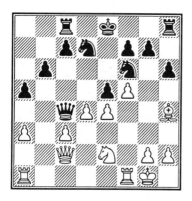

19.de5! (Here the sprint to g7 begins) **19...♕e4 20.ef6!!** (A Queen sacrifice that shook the chess world, but a necessary element of this well-planned combination) **20...♕c2 21.fg7** (For the Queen White gets only a Bishop, but the opponenet's King is in danger. The following moves of Black are forced) **21...♖g8 22.♘d4 ♕e4 23.♖ae1 ♘c5 24.♖e4 ♘e4 25.♖e1** (Now White gets a decisive material advantage) **25...♖g7 26.♖e4 ♔d7** (Not waiting for the obvious 27.♖e7 ♔d6 28.f6 ♖g4 29.♗g3 +–, Black resigns), **1-0**

An analogous idea was put into practice by the "Magician from Riga," ex-world champion Mikhail Tal, during the 15th chess Olympiad at Varna.

Game 8
Tal,M—Hecht,H
Varna 1962

1.d4 ♘f6 2.c4 e6 3.♘f3 b6 4.♘c3 ♗b4 5.♗g5 ♗b7 6.e3 h6 7.♗h4 ♗c3 8.bc3 d6 9.♘d2 e5 10.f3 ♕e7 11.e4 ♘bd7 12.♗d3 ♘f8 13.c5 dc5 14.de5 ♕e5 15.♕a4 c6? (△ 15...♘6d7) **16.0-0 ♘g6 17.♘c4 ♕e6** (Now the Steeplechase begins its e4-e5-f6-g7 route. Further comments are by Tal, with some abridgement)

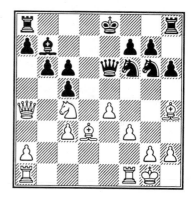

18.e5! (White's main goal is to keep the enemy King on e8. The combination begins in the hope of securing the more advantageous ending – nothing more is expected from this position) **18...b5** (There was an interesting continuation in 18...♘h4!?, for after 19.♘d6 ♔f8 it is disadvantageous for White to take any of the three pieces threatened. For example, if 20.♘b7 or 20.♕h4, then 20...♕e5. However, White has the positional 20.♖fe1!, as Black would find it impossible to protect all three pieces) **19.ef6!!** (Now most players of Black would happily go 19...0-0, for then three White pieces would be under fire, and if 20.♕c2 ♘h4 then Black is under no pressure at all. However, let's not forget about vigilance! For after 19...0-0 White has a very strong argument – and even stronger attack – with 20.♖fe1!. After 20...♕d5 could follow 21.♕c2 ♘h4 22.♘e5 with a strong attack; or if 20...♕e1 21.♖e1 ba4 22.♗g6 fg6 23.♖e7, and Black cannot continue with 23...♖f7? because of 24.♘d6) **19...ba4 20.fg7 ♖g8**

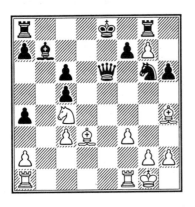

21.♗f5!! (The climax of the combination! After 21...♕c4 Black has a spare Queen, but still would lose after 22.♖fe1 ♕e6 23.♖e6 fe6 24.♗g6 ♔d7 25.♖d1 ♔c7 26.♗g3 ♔b6 27.♖b1 ♔a6 28.♗d3 ♔a5 29.♗c7#. The try 21...♕f5 leads to a hopeless ending for Black after 22.♘d6 ♔d7 23.♘f5 ♘h4 24.♖ad1 ♔c7 25.♘h4 ♖g7 26.♖fe1 +−) **21...♘h4 22.♗e6 ♗a6** (How to save one of the pieces? The variation

22...fe6 23.♘d6 ♔d7 24.♘b7 illustrates dexterity of the White Knight) **23.♘d6 ♔e7 24.♗c4!** (The combination is completed, bringing a weighty advantage in the ending to White) **24...♖g7 25.g3 ♔d6** (Black had a chance to escape the worst by 25...♗c4 26.♘c4 ♖d8) **26.♗a6 ♘f5 27.♖ab1 f6 28.♖fd1 ♔e7 29.♖e1 ♔d6 30.♔f2 c4 31.g4 ♘e7 32.♖b7 ♖ag8 33.♗c4 ♘d5 34.♗d5 cd5 35.♖b4 ♖c8** (It would be better to exchange Kingside pawns with 35...h5 36.h3 hg4 37.hg4 f5, but even that could hardly help) **36.♖a4 ♖c3 37.♖a6 ♔c5 38.♖f6 h5 39.h3 hg4 40.hg4 ♖h7 41.g5 ♖h5 42.♖f5 ♖c2 43.♔g3 ♔c4 44.♖ee5! d4 45.g6 ♖h1 46.♖c5 ♔d3 47.♖c2 ♔c2 48.♔f4 ♖g1 49.♖g5** (Black resigned in view of 49...♖g5 50.♔g5 d3 51.g7 d2 52.g8=♕ d1=♕ 53.♕b3 +−), **1-0** (M.Tal)

In conclusion, let's consider another Steeplechase, a performance by the chief priestess of Caissa's temple, the unmatched Judit Polgar. It is a "quick-play" game from Geneva.

Game 9
Polgar,J–Epishin,V
Geneva 1996

1.e4 c6 2.d4 d5 3.♘c3 de4 4.♘e4 ♘d7 5.♗c4 ♘gf6 6.♘g5 e6 7.♕e2 ♘b6 8.♗b3 h6

9.♘5f3 c5 10.♗f4 ♗d6 11.♗g3
♕c7 12.dc5 ♕c5 13.0-0-0 ♗g3
14.hg3 ♗d7 15.♖h4 ♖c8
16.♘e5 ♗b5 17.♕e1 0-0
18.♘gf3 ♘bd5 19.♔b1 ♗c6
20.♕d2 ♖fe8 (20...♖fd8 21.♖dh1
♕f8 22.g4 ±, J.Polgar) 21.♖dh1
♕f8

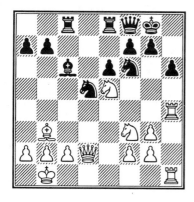

22.g4 (It is hard to imagine, but
this pawn will reach the h7-square
in 4 moves!) 22...♘e4 23.♕e1 (A
forced intermediate move) 23...♘d6
24.g5 ♘f5 25.gh6 ♘h4 26.h7
♔h8 (Judit has ushered the pawn
to its goal; now there follows a
mating attack. The remaining notes
are from J.Polgar in Inf. 67/180)
27.♘h4 (27.♘g5 ♖e7 28.♖h4
♗e8) 27...♘f4 (27...♘e7 28.♗e6)
28.♕b4! g5 (28...♕b4 29.♘hg6
fg6 30.♘f7#) 29.♕d4 ♔g7
(29...♕g7 30.♘hg6 fg6 31.♘f7#)
30.♘f5 ef5 31.h8=♕ ♕h8
32.♘f7, 1-0

Alexander Alekhine Plays the Steeplechase

Game 10

Blumenfeld, B—Alekhine, A
Moscow 1908

1.e4 e5 2.♘f3 d6 3.d4 ♘d7 (△
3...♘f6 4.de5 ♘e4 5.♗c4 c6 =)
4.b3 (4.♗c4 c6 5.♘c3 ♗e7 6.de5
de5 7.♘g5! ♗g5 8.♕h5! ±) 4...c6
5.♗b2 ♕c7 6.♘bd2 (△ 7.♘c4)
6...♘e7 (△ 7...♘g6, × e5,f4) 7.♗e2
(△ 7.g3, △ 8.♗g2) 7...♘g6 8.0-0
♗e7 9.a4?! 0-0 10.♘c4 ♖d8 (× d
⇔) 11.♕c1 (△ 11.♖e1, △ 12.♗f1)
11...♘f4 12.♖e1 ♘e2 13.♖e2 f6
14.♘h4 ♘f8 (△ ...♘e6, ...♘f4)
15.♘e3 ♘e6 16.de5 (16.♘ef5
♗f8 17.c3 g6 18.♘g3 ♘f4 19.♖d2
♗e6 20.♕c2 ♕f7 ∓) 16...de5
17.♘hf5 ♗b4! (△ 18...♘f4)
18.c3 (18.g3 ♘g5; 18.f3 ♘f4
19.♖f2 ♗f5 20.ef5 [20.♘f5 ♗c5
21.♘e3 ♕b6 22.a5! ♗e3 23.ab6
♗c1 24.♖c1 ab6 ∓] 20...♗c5, △
21...♘d5, 22...♕b6) 18...♘f4
(18...♗f8 19.♖d2 ♘f4 20.♖d8 ♕d8
[20...♘e2 21.♔f1 ♘c1 22.♖f8 ♔f8
23.♗a3 ♔f7 24.♖c1] 21.♕d1)
19.♖d2 ♗f5 20.♘f5 ♗c5 21.b4
♗f8 22.♖d8 ♖d8 23.♕c2 ♕d7
24.♖f1 ♕d3! 25.♕b3 (25.♕d3
♖d3 26.♘g3 c5 27.bc5 ♗c5, △
28...♖d2) 25...♔h8 26.♘g3

26...h5 (The h-pawn begins its victory march. Yet Alekhine saw another way to win the game, by 26...♘e2 27.♘e2 ♕e2 28.♗c1 ♕e4 29.♕f7 c5 30.bc5 ♗c5 31.♕c7 ♗b6 –+, V.Ch.) **27.♗c1** (△ 27.h4! ♘e2 [27...g5 28.♕f7 ♗g7 29.hg5 fg5 30.♗c1] 28.♘e2 ♕e2 29.♗c1 ♕e4 30.♕f7 c5! 31.♕h5 ♔g8 ∓) **27...h4! 28.♗f4 ef4 29.♘f5 h3!** (29...♕e4 30.♘h4) **30.♕e6** (30.gh3 ♕e4 31.♘d4 ♖d5! 32.f3 ♕e3!; 30.f3 ♕e2! 31.gh3 ♖d2; 30.♖e1 ♕d2! 31.♖f1 ♕e2 –+) **30...hg2 31.♔g2** (31.♖e1 ♕c3 32.♖b1 ♕c2 33.♖e1 ♖d1 34.♖d1 ♕d1 35.♔g2 ♕g4 36.♔f1 ♗b4 37.♕c8 ♔h7 38.♕b7 a5 39.♕c6 f3! –+) **31...f3 32.♔g1 ♕f1, 0–1** (A.Alekhine)

Game 11
Alekhine,A—Levitsky,S
St. Petersburg 1913

1.e4 e5 2.f4 ef4 3.♗c4 ♘f6
(3...♕h4 4.♔f1 d5 5.♗d5 g5 6.g3

fg3 7.♕f3!, M.Chigorin) **4.♘c3 ♗b4** (4...c6!?) **5.♘ge2** (5.♘f3 0-0 6.0-0 ♘e4 7.♘d5!; 7.♘e4 d5 =) **5...d5** (5...♘e4 6.0-0) **6.ed5 f3 7.gf3 0-0 8.d4** (8.0-0! c6 9.dc6 ♘c6 10.d4 ♗h3 11.♖f2 ♖c8 ∞) **8...♗h3** (8...♘d5 9.0-0 ♗e6 =) **9.♗g5** (9.♘f4 ♖e8 10.♔f2 ♘g4! 11.♔g3 ♘f2 –+) **9...♗g2 10.♖g1 ♗f3 11.♕d2** (△ 12.♕f4) **11...♗e7** (11...♘e4 12.♗d8 ♘d2 13.♗f6; 11...♗e2 12.♗e2 ♗c3 13.♕c3 ♖e8 14.0-0-0 ♖e2 15.♕f3) **12.0-0-0 ♗h5** (12...♘e4 13.♗e7 ♘d2 [13...♕e7 14.♕h6!] 14.♗d8 ♘c4 15.♖g7 ♔g7 16.♖g1 ♔h6 17.♗g5 ♔g6 [17...♔h5 18.♘f4#] 18.♗e7 ♔f5 19.♗f8) **13.♖de1 ♘bd7 14.♘f4 ♗g6 15.h4!** (△ 16.h5) **15...♖e8 16.♕g2** (△ 17.h5) **16...♗f8 17.h5 ♗f5**

18.♘e6! fe6 (18...♕c8 19.♕f3! +–) **19.de6** (The d-pawn Steeplechase. V.Ch.) **19...♔h8 20.ed7 ♖e1**

**21.♖e1 ♗d7 22.h6 +− ♗c6
23.d5 ♗d7 24.♖f1 b5 25.♗b3
♕e8 26.d6** (26.♖f6) **26...♘h5**
(26...♗c6 27.d7 [Another Steeplechase! V.Ch.] 27...♗g2 [27...♕d7
28.♕f2 ♘g8 29.♕f8!] 28.de8=♕
♖e8 29.♖f6) **27.♗f7 ♕e5
28.♕a8, 1-0** (A.Alekhine)

Game 12
Alekhine, A—Grigoriev, N
Moscow 1915

**1.e4 e6 2.d4 d5 3.♘c3 ♘f6
4.♗g5** (4.ed5 ed5 5.♗g5 ♘c6!? =)
4...♗b4 5.e5 h6 6.ef6
("Chigorin's Steeplechase," VCh;
6.♗d2 ♗c3 7.bc3 ♘e4 8.♕g4 ♔f8!)
**6...hg5 7.fg7 ♖g8 8.h4 gh4
9.♕g4** (Grigoriev; 9.♕h5?!)
9...♗e7 10.g3! c5 (△ 10...♗f6)
**11.gh4 cd4 12.h5! dc3 13.h6
cb2** (Black answers with a Steeplechase along the path c7-c5-
d4-c3-b2, V.Ch.) **14.♖b1 ♕a5
15.♔e2 ♕a2 16.h7 ♕b1
17.hg8=♕** (Wonderful! The third
Steeplechase in this game. V.Ch.)
**17...♔d7 18.♕f7 ♕c2 19.♔f3
♘c6 20.♕ge6 ♔c7 21.♕f4 ♔b6
22.♕ee3 ♗c5 23.g8=♕** (?
23.♗d3!! +−, V.Ch.) **23...b1=♕**

(see next diagram)

24.♖h6!! (△ 25.♕d8#) **24...♕f1**
(24...♗g4! =) **25.♕b4 ♕b5**

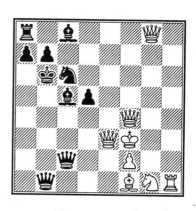

After 23...b1=♕

26.♕d8 ♔a6 27.♕ea3, 1-0
(A.Alekhine)

Game 13
Alekhine, A—Hofmeister
Petrograd 1917 (♘b1 odds)

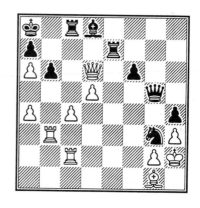

1.c5 b5 (1...♘f1 2.♔h1 ♘g3
3.♖g3! ♕g3 4.cb6! ♖c2 [4...♕d6
5.♖c8 ♕b8 6.b7! ♖b7 7.ab7 ♔b7
8.♖b8 ♔b8 9.♗f2 ±; 4...♖ec7
5.♖c7 +−; 4...♖b8 5.b7 +−] 5.♕d8
♕b8 6.♕e7 ab6 7.♕f6 ±; 1...♖e2
[△ 2...♘f1] 2.♖e2 ♘e2, △ 3...♗c7

∓; 1...♘e4 2.cb6! ♕g2!! 3.♖g2 ♘d6 4.b7 ♘b7 5.ab7 ♖b7 6.♖b7 ♔b7 7.♖g7 ♖c7 8.♖g4 f5 9.♖b4 ♔a8 10.♖f4 ±) **2.ab5 ♘e4** (2...♖e3 3.♖e2 ♘e2 4.b6! +−; 2...♘f1 3.♔h1 ♘g3 4.♖g3 ♕g3 5.b6! ab6 [5...♕d6 6.cd6 ♖c2 7.de7 ♗e7 8.b7 ♔b8 9.♗h2 ♖c7 10.♗f4 ♗c5 11.g3 hg3 12.h4 ♗d4 13.♗c7 ♔c7 14.d6 ♔b8 15.d7 ♗b6 16.h5 +−] 6.cb6 ♕d6 7.♖c8 ♕b8 8.b7 ♖b7 9.ab7 ♔b7 10.♖b8 ♔b8 ±) **3.b6! ♘d6** (3...ab6 4.cb6 ♕g2 5.♖g2 ♘d6 6.b7 ♘b7 7.ab7 ♖b7 8.♖a2 ♔b8 9.♗a7 ♔a8 [9...♔c7 10.♖c2 ♔d6 11.♖c8 ♖b3 12.♖d8] 10.♖ba3! ±) **4.cd6 ♖ec7** (4...♖c2 5.b7 ♖b7 6.ab7 ♔b8 7.♗a7 +−; 4...♖b8 5.b7 +−; 4...ab6 5.♖c8 ♔a7 6.de7 ♕f4 7.♔h1 ♗e7 8.♗b6 ♔a6 9.♖a8 ♔b7 10.♗e3; 4...♗c7 5.b7 ♔b8 6.dc7 ♖ec7 [6...♖cc7 7.♗a7] 7.♖c7! ♕e5 8.♔h1! ♔c7 [8...♕c7 9.♗h2; 8...♖c7 9.♗a7] 9.♗h2 ±) **5.b7** (The Steeplechase route: a4-b5-b6-b7!, V.Ch.) **5...♔b8 6.d7!! ♕g3 7.♔h1, 1-0** (A.Kotov)

We cannot resist showing the final position. A fantastic combination!

Game 14
Alekhine,A—Novak
Praha 1925

1.d4 g6 2.e4 ♗g7 3.♘f3 c5 4.c3 cd4 5.cd4 ♘c6 6.d5 ♘e5 7.♘c3 a6 8.♗f4 ♘f3 9.♕f3 e5 (9...d6) **10.de6 fe6 11.0-0-0 ♘e7 12.♗d6 b5 13.e5 ♖a7 14.♗d3 ♘c6?** (△ 14...♗b7) **15.♕g3 ♘e7** (15...♗b7?? 16.♕g6 hg6 17.♗g6#) **16.h4** (A Steeplechase begins along the path h2-h4-h5-g6-h7! V.Ch.) **16...♖f8 17.h5 ♗h6 18.♔b1 ♘f5**

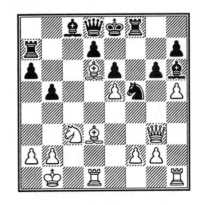

19.hg6!! (19.♗f5 gf5 20.♗f8 ♔f8 ⩱) **19...♘g3 20.gh7** (△ 21.♗g6) **20...♔f7** (20...♘f5 21.♗f8, △ 22.h8=♕) **21.fg3 ♔g7 22.♗f8 ♕f8 23.♖df1 ♕h8** (23...♕f1 24.♖f1 ♔h8 25.♘e4!, △ 26.♘d6 +−) **24.♖f6 d5 25.♖hh6, 1-0** (A.Alekhine)

Game 15
Alekhine,A—Te Kolste,J
Baden Baden 1925

1.d4 d5 2.c4 c6 3.♘c3 ♘f6 4.e3 e6 5.♘f3 ♘bd7 6.♗d3 dc4 7.♗c4 b5 8.♗d3 a6 9.e4! c5 10.e5 ♘d5 (△ 10...cd4 11.♘b5 [= 11.♘e4] 11...♘e5) **11.♘g5** (11.♘d5 ed5 12.dc5 ♘c5 13.♘d4) **11...cd4 12.♘d5!** (12.♘e6 ♕a5!) **12...ed5 13.0-0 ♗e7?** (13...♘c5! 14.f4)

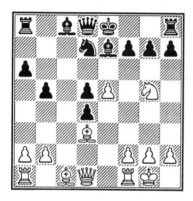

14.e6! ♘e5 (14...♗g5 15.♕h5!) **15.ef7** (A short but effective Steeplechase! V.Ch.) **15...♔f8** (15...♘f7 16.♖e1 +−) **16.♘h7 ♔f7 17.♕h5! g6 18.♕e5 ♖h7 19.♕d4 ♖h4** (19...♗f6 20.♕c5) **20.♕e3 ♕h8 21.♗g6 ♔g6 22.♕e7 ♖a7 23.♕a7 ♖h2 24.♕b6 ♔f5 25.g4!, 1-0** (A.Alekhine)

Game 16
Alekhine,A—Treybal,K
Semmering 1926

1.d4 d5 2.c4 c6 3.e3 (3.♘f3) **3...e6 4.♗d3 f5 5.♕c2 ♕f6** (5...♘d7 6.cd5; 5...♘f6 6.f3, △ ♘e2, ♘bc3, ♗d2, 0-0-0, e3-e4) **6.♘c3 ♗d7** (6...♗d6? 7.cd5 ed5 8.♘d5; 6...♘a6 7.a3 ♘c7 8.♘f3 ♗d6 9.c5) **7.♘f3 ♗d6 8.a3 ♘h6** (8...♘a6 9.c5, △ 10.♗a6) **9.b3** (9.b4 0-0 10.e4! fe4 11.♗e4 de4 12.♘e4 ♕e7 13.♗g5) **9...♘f7 10.♗b2 g6** (10...♕e7 11.h3) **11.h3 ♕e7** (11...0-0 12.0-0-0, △ 13.g4 fg4 14.♘d2!) **12.b4! dc4** (12...♘g5 13.♘g5 ♕g5 14.g3, △ 15.h4; 12...0-0 13.g4) **13.♗c4 b5 14.♗b3 a5 15.ba5 ♘a6** (15...♖a5 16.e4! ♗a3 17.0-0! ♗b4 18.♖a5 ♗a5 19.d5 +−) **16.e4!** (16.0-0 g5!) **16...0-0 17.0-0 ♘g5 18.♘g5 ♕g5 19.e5!** (19.d5 cd5 20.♘d5 [20.ed5 e5] 20...♖ac8) **19...♗e7** (19...♗c7 20.d5!)

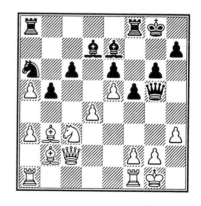

20.d5! (Another d-pawn Steeplechase. V.Ch.) **20...♘c5** (20...cd5

21.♘d5 ♖ac8 [21...ed5 22.♗d5 +−] 22.♕d1 +−) **21.de6 ♘b3** (21...♗e6 22.♗e6 ♘e6 23.♕b3 ♔f7 24.♘e2 c5 25.♗c1 c4 26.♕b5; 21...♘e6 22.♖ad1 ♗c8 23.♘e2) **22.ed7!** (22.♕b3 ♗c8 23.♖ad1; 23.f4 ♕h6, △ 24...g5) **22...♘a1 23.♖a1 ♖fd8 24.♖d1** (24.e6 ♗f6 [24...f4 25.♘b5 ♕b5 26.♕c3] 25.♕b3 ♔f8 26.♖e1) **24...♕h4 25.e6 b4!** (25...h6 26.♘b5 cb5 27.♕c3) **26.ab4 ♕b4 27.♘e2 ♖a5 28.♘d4 ♖c5 29.♕e2 ♕c4** (29...h6 30.♘c6 ♖c6 31.♕e5; 29...♕a4 30.♖d2, △ ♕e3-h6 +−) **30.♗a3 ♕e2 31.♘e2 ♖d5 32.♖d5 ♗a3 33.♖d3 ♗c5 34.♘d4, 1−0** (A.Alekhine)

Game 17
Carransa,L—Alekhine,A
Buenos Aires 1926

1.e4 e5 2.♘f3 ♘c6 3.♗b5 a6 4.♗a4 ♘f6 5.0-0 d6 6.d4 ♗d7 (6...b5 7.♗b3 [7.de5] 7...♘d4 8.♘d4 ed4 9.c3!) **7.♖e1 b5 8.♗b3** (8.de5 de5 9.♗b3 ♗d6 10.♗g5 h6 =) **8...♘d4 9.♘d4 ed4 10.e5** (10.c3 dc3 11.♘c3 ♗e7 ∓) **10...de5 11.♖e5 ♗e7** (11...♗e6 12.♗e6 fe6 13.♖e6 ♔f7) **12.♕e1 c5** (12...♔f8, △ ...♗d6, ...c5) **13.♗d2** (13.♖c5? 0-0) **13...a5 14.a4 c4 15.ab5** (15.♗a2! ♘g4! 16.♖e2 [16.♖e4 ♗f5 17.♖e2 ♗e6] 16...♗e6 17.h3 [17.ab5 ♕b8!] 17...♘f6

18.ab5 0-0 19.♘a3 ♗a3 20.ba3 ±) **15...cb3 16.♗a5**

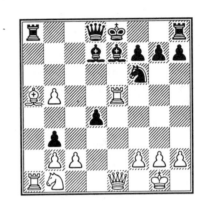

16...bc2! (A fantastic c7-c5-c4-b3-c2 Steeplechase! V.Ch.) **17.♗d8 ♖a1 18.♖e7 ♔d8, 0-1** (A.Alekhine)

Game 18
Alekhine,A—Veenink,H
Prague 1931

1.d4 d5 2.c4 c6 3.♘f3 ♘f6 4.e3 ♗f5 5.cd5 ♗b1? (5...cd5 6.♕b3 ♕c7) **6.♖b1 ♕d5 7.a3** (7.♕c2 ♕a2 [7...e6 8.b4!] 8.♗c4 ♕a5 9.♗d2 ♕c7 10.e4) **7...e6 8.♕c2 ♗e7** (8...c5 9.b4!) **9.♗d3 h6** (9...0-0 10.e4, △ 11.e5) **10.e4 ♕d8 11.0-0 ♘bd7 12.b4!** (△ 13.♖b3) **12...0-0 13.♕e2 ♖e8 14.♖b3! ♕c7 15.♗b1 ♘h7** (15...a5 16.♕c2 ♘f8 17.b5) **16.e5 f5** (16...♘hf8 17.g4!) **17.ef6 ♗f6 18.♕e4 ♘hf8 19.♕g4** (△ 20.♗h6) **19...♔h8 20.♕h5 ♘h7 21.♖e1 ♖ad8** (In this position the world champion rips open the enemy King's fortress with a g-pawn march [V.Ch.]. Instead, if 21...e5 then 22.♗f4!)

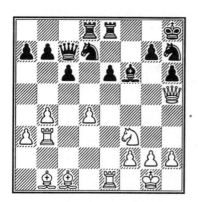

22.g4! ♕d6 23.♗g6! (23.g5 ♕d5) 23...♖f8 24.g5 ♗d4 25.gh6 ♘df6 26.hg7 ♔g7 27.♕h6 ♔h8 (27...♔g8 28.♘d4 ♕d4 29.♖g3) 28.♘d4 ♕d4 29.♗b2! (29...♕d7 □ 30.♖d3! ♕g7 31.♗f6!), 1-0 (A.Alekhine)

Game 19
Peres—Alekhine, A
Madrid 1943 (blitz)

1.e4 e5 2.♘c3 ♘c6 3.f4 ef4 4.♘f3 g5 5.d4 g4 6.♗c4 gf3 7.♗f4 fg2

(see next diagram)

(The World Champion is playing blitz games versus the participants in the Madrid 1943 tournament. Here Alekhine has fallen into a terrible trap) 8.♗f7 ♔f7 9.♕h5 ♔g7 10.♖g1 ♘ge7 11.♗h6 ♔g8 12.♖g2, 1-0

After 7...fg2

Game 20
Alekhine, A—Saemisch, F
Berlin 1923 (blindfold)

1.e4 c5 2.♘f3 ♘c6 3.♗e2 e6 4.0-0 d6 5.d4 cd4 6.♘d4 ♘f6 7.♗f3 ♘e5 8.c4 ♘f3 9.♕f3 ♗e7 10.♘c3 0-0 11.b3 ♘d7 12.♗b2 ♗f6 13.♖ad1 a6 14.♕g3 ♕c7 15.♔h1 ♖d8 16.f4 b6 17.f5 ♗e5

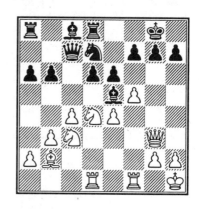

18.fe6!! ♗g3 19.ef7 ♔h8 20.♘d5!! (20...♕a7 21.♘c6 ♗e5 22.♗e5 de5 23.♘a7 ♖a7 24.♘b6

♖f8 25.♘c8 ♖c8 26.♖d7 +– ;
20...♕b7 21.♘e6 ♗e5 22.♘d8 +– ;
20...♕c5 21.♘e6 ♗e5 22.♗e5 de5
23.♘c5 bc5 24.♘c7 ♖b8 25.♘e8!!
+– ; 20...♕b8 21.♘c6 ♗e5
[21...♕b7 22.♘d8] 22.♗e5 de5
23.♘b8 ♖b8 24.♘c7 ♖f8 25.♘e6,
△ 26.♘f8 ♘f8 27.♖d8 +–), **1-0**
(A.Alekhine)

Game 21
Alekhine,A—Gize
corr. 1906

1.e4 e5 2.♘c3 ♘f6 3.f4 d5 4.fe5
♘e4 5.♕f3 f5 6.♘ge2 ♘c6 7.d4
♘b4 8.♔d1 c5 9.♘f4 g6 10.♗b5
♗d7 11.♗d7 ♕d7 12.♗e3 ♗h6
13.♘d3 ♘d3 14.cd3 ♘c3 15.bc3
♗e3 16.♕e3 ♕a4 17.♔d2 cd4
18.♕d4 ♕d4 19.cd4 ♖c8 20.♖hc1
♔d7 21.♔e3 ♖c1 22.♖c1 ♖c8??

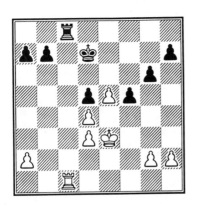

23.e6! ♔d8 24.e7 ♔d7 25.♖c8
(25...♔c8 26.e8=♕ +–), 1-0

This game was the foundation for
Game 1 (p.10).

Laws of the Steeplechase

From the games and analysis featur-
ing this combination, we may draw a
number of conclusions:

1. The primary goal of the Steeplechase combination is to reach the
7th rank (or even the 8th, upon oc-
casion) with a pawn.

2. The further back from this goal
the Steeplechase begins, the more
spectacular the combination. That's
why, in the case of a Steeplechase beginning on the 5th rank, the pawn
must race to the target square and re-
main there for at least one move.

To elaborate this point, in cases
where the pawn perishes at the end
of its journey, then the combination
turns into a simple exchange.

For example, if on the White pawn's
route d5-d6-c7 Black now plays
...♗c7, then it's only an exchange
combination. But playing d5-c6-b7
answered by ...♖b8, or d5-d6-d7

answered by ...♖d8, gives us a true Steeplechase.

3. Any intermediate moves lessen the esthetic impression. The number of intermediate moves must therefore be limited. Here we suggest the simplest formula: $N + M < 5$, where N = the numbered rank from which the pawn starts, and M = the number of intermediate moves. So, when starting from the second rank, no more than three intermediate moves are allowed ($2 + 3 = 5$). The analogous formula for Black is $N - M > 4$, i.e. when Black starts from the sixth rank there must be no more than two intermediate moves ($6 - 2 = 4$).

4. The number of direct or indirect obstacles must not be less than two. In the diagram above, the White pawn overcomes two indirect obstacles along the d5-d6-d7 route – the Black pawns on c6 and c7. On the path d5-c6-b7 two direct obstacles are surmounted – the pawns c6 and b7. In other words, direct obstacles are to be overcome by capture, and indirect obstacles by avoiding them.

The Steeplechase is often accompanied by the sacrifice of pawns and pieces, which makes the combination even more spectacular.

Part Two

The Opening Steeplechase

The Steeplechase is one of the few combinational types seen regularly in chess openings. Sometimes it is merely a kind of trap, but more often it's a positional method of piece development or the means to secure an opening advantage. The following review is incomplete – more openings that feature the Steeplechase could be demonstrated. Some systems have become quietly antiquated, or were incorrect from the beginning. However, the sample size is large enough to prove our point, that the Steeplechase is clearly one of the basic tactical elements, like those illustrated in *The Tactician's Handbook*. The openings are examined below in the order of their ECO code.

Paris Opening [A00]

Game 22
Myers,H—Alvarez
Santo Domingo 1966

1.♘h3 d5 2.g3 e5 3.f4 (Black's e5-pawn is invited to a Steeplechase,

aiming for the h2-square) **3...♗h3** (Black accepts the challenge) **4.♗h3 ef4 5.0-0 fg3 6.e4** (The idea of this opening belongs to S.Tartakower, who introduced it in the 1930s. One of his games continued instead 6.hg3 ♘f6 7.d3 ♘c6 8.♘c3 ♗d6 9.♗g5 ♗g3 10.♗f6 gf6 11.e4 ♖g8 12.♘d5 ♗e5 13.♔h1 ♕d6 14.c3 ♖g3 15.♕h5 ♖d3 16.♖ad1 ♖d1 17.♖d1 ♘e7 18.♘e3 ♕c5 19.♕h7 +–, 1-0. Tartakower–Lilienthal, Paris 1933) **6...gh2 7.♔h1** (A typical position. In shedding three pawns, White achieved not only a great advantage in development and an attacking position, but can also use the Black h2-pawn as a shield for his own King!)

7...de4 (A delicate hint: Black's e-pawn is ready to begin its own Steeplechase to the c2-square. Myers allows the charge, and establishes a record by sacrificing 6 pawns in the opening!) **8.♘c3 ♘f6 9.d3!?** **ed3 10.♗g5 dc2 11.♕f3** (A unique case – both Black center pawns have marched to the second rank within ten moves. As a result, White developed his pieces and will deliver mate in seven more moves)

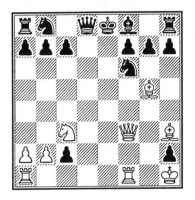

11...♗e7 12.♕b7 ♘bd7 13.♗d7 ♘d7 14.♗e7 ♔e7 15.♘d5 ♔f8 16.♘c7 ♘c5 17.♘e6 ♘e6 18.♕f7#, 1-0

Game 23
Garnett—Muller
Guernsey 1980

1.♘h3 e5 2.g3 d5 3.f4 ♗h3 4.♗h3 ef4 5.0-0 fg3 6.e4 gh2 7.♔h1 de4 8.d3 ♘f6 9.♘c3 ed3 10.♗g5 ♗e7 11.♕f3 0-0 12.♖ae1 ♘c6 13.♕g2 ♘h5 14.♗e7 ♘e7 15.♗g4 d2 16.♖e5 ♘f6 17.♖f6 gf6 18.♖d5 ♕b8 19.♖h5 ♔g7 20.♕d2 ♖h8 21.♕h6 ♔g8 22.♘e4, 1-0

Larsen's Opening [A00]

Game 24
Schussler,H—Huss,A
Buenos Aires 1978

1.b3 c5 2.♗b2 ♘c6 3.♘f3 ♘f6 4.e3 e6 5.c4 b6 6.♘c3 ♗b7 7.♗e2 ♗e7 8.0-0 0-0 9.d4 d5 (The beginning moves of a mutual Steeplechase, which unexpectedly leads to a draw!)

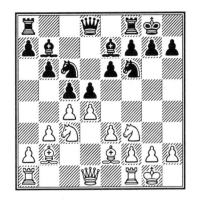

10.dc5 dc4 11.cb6 cb3 12.ba7 ba2 (Mirror-image moves from beginning to end!) **13.♖a2 ♕d1 14.♖d1 ♖a7 15.♖a7 ♘a7, 1/2-1/2**

English Opening [A18]

On the third move of this variation there begins a simultaneous Steeplechase with obstacles. White's route is e2-e4-e5-f6-g7; Black's route is d7-d5-d4-e3-d2.

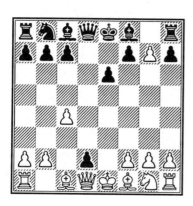

After 1.c4 ♘f6 2.♘c3 e6 3.e4 d5 4.e5 d4 5.ef6 dc3 6.fg7 cd2

Game 25
Nimzowitsch,A—Nillson,B
Copenhagen 1933

1.c4 ♘f6 2.♘c3 e6 3.e4 d5 4.e5 d4 5.ef6 dc3 6.fg7 cd2 7.♗d2 ♗g7 8.♕c2 ♘c6 9.♘f3 ♘d4 10.♘d4 ♗d4 11.♗d3 ♕f6 12.0-0 ♗d7 13.♗e4 0-0-0 14.♗c3 e5 15.♗d4 ed4 16.♕d3 ♗c6 17.f3 h5 18.♖ae1 h4 19.♗f5 ♔b8 20.b4 ♖h5 21.♗g4 ♖hh8 22.b5 ♗d7 23.♗d7 ♖d7 24.a4 ♕g6 25.♕g6 fg6 26.♖e6 ♖g8 27.♔f2 d3 28.♖d1 b6 29.♖d2 g5 30.h3 ♖gd8 31.♔e3 ♖d4 32.♖e8 ♖e8 33.♔d4 ♖d8 34.♔c3 ♖e8 35.♖d3 ♖e2 36.♖d2 ♖e3 37.♔d4 ♖e1 38.♔d5 c5 39.♔d6 ♔b7 40.♖d5 ♖c1 41.♖g5 ♖c4 42.♖g7 ♔c8 43.♖a7, 1-0

Game 26
Ragozin,V—Sozin,V
Leningrad 1934

1.c4 ♘f6 2.♘c3 e6 3.e4 d5 4.e5 d4 5.ef6 dc3 6.fg7 cd2 7.♗d2 ♗g7 8.♕c2 c5 9.♘f3 ♘c6 10.♗d3 ♘d4 11.♘d4 ♗d4 12.0-0-0 h5 13.♖he1 ♗d7 14.♗e3 ♕a5 15.♗e4 0-0-0 16.♗d4 cd4 17.♕b3 ♗c6 18.♗c6 bc6 19.♕f3 ♖d6 20.♔b1 ♕c7 21.♖e4 ♕d7 22.♕f6 ♖d8 23.♖d3 ♕c7 24.♖e5 h4 25.♕h4 ♖g8 26.g3 ♖dd8 27.♕e4 ♕d7 28.♖c5 ♔c7 29.♖a3 ♔d6 30.♖ca5, 1-0

Game 27
Ragozin,V—Makogonov,V
Leningrad 1939

1.c4 ♘f6 2.♘c3 e6 3.e4 d5 4.e5 d4 5.ef6 dc3 6.fg7 cd2 7.♗d2 ♗g7 8.♕c2 c5 9.♗c3 ♗c3 10.♕c3 ♖g8 11.♖d1 ♕e7 12.♗d3 f5 13.♗e2 ♘c6 14.♗h5 ♔f8 15.♘e2 e5 16.0-0 ♗e6 17.f4 e4 18.♖d2 ♖d8 19.b3 ♕h4 20.♖d8 ♕d8 21.♕e3 b6 22.♘c3 ♕d4 23.♖e1 ♖g7 24.♘b5 ♕b2 25.♕e2 ♕f6 26.♖d1 ♘d4 27.♘d4 cd4 28.♕b2 ♖d7 29.♕a3 ♔g8 30.♗e8 ♖d8 31.♗c6 d3 32.♕a7 e3 33.♗f3 e2 34.♗e2 ♕d4, 0-1

Game 28
Tartakower,S—List,P
London 1946

1.c4 ♘f6 2.♘c3 e6 3.e4 d5 4.e5 d4
5.ef6 dc3 6.fg7 cd2 7.♗d2 ♗g7
8.♕c2 c5 9.0-0-0 ♕c7 10.♗c3 e5
11.f4 ♘c6 12.fe5 0-0 13.♘f3 ♖d8
14.♖d8 ♕d8 15.♕e4 ♘d4 16.♗d4
cd4 17.♗d3 h6 18.♖e1 ♗e6
19.♘d4 ♗c4 20.♗c4 ♖c8 21.♘c2
b5 22.♗b3 ♖c5 23.e6 fe6 24.♕e6
♚h8 25.♕f7, 1-0

Game 29
Cherepkov,A—Osmolovsky,M
Moscow 1949

1.c4 ♘f6 2.♘c3 e6 3.e4 d5 4.e5 d4
5.ef6 dc3 6.fg7 cd2 7.♗d2 ♗g7
8.♕c2 c5 9.♘f3 ♘c6 10.♗d3 f5
11.0-0-0 ♗d7 12.g4 fg4 13.♗h7 gf3
14.♕g6 ♚f8 15.♗h6 ♕f6 16.♕f6,
1-0

Game 30
Dvorzinsky—Stein
Poland 1966

1.c4 ♘f6 2.♘c3 e6 3.e4 d5 4.e5 d4
5.ef6 dc3 6.fg7 cd2 7.♗d2 ♗g7
8.♕c2 ♘c6 9.♘f3 ♗d7 10.♗d3
♕e7 11.♗h7 0-0-0 12.♗e4 f5
13.♗c6 ♗c6 14.0-0-0 ♗e4 15.♗g5
♗h6 16.♖d8 ♖d8 17.♗h6 ♗c2
18.♗g5 ♕c5 19.♗d8 ♚d8 20.♚c2
♕f2 21.♚c3 ♕g2 22.♖d1 ♚e7, 0-1

Game 31
Roizman,A—Boleslavsky,I
Minsk 1957

1.c4 ♘f6 2.♘c3 e6 3.e4 d5 4.e5 d4
5.ef6 dc3 6.fg7 cd2 7.♗d2 ♗g7
8.♕c2 ♘c6 9.♘f3 ♕e7 10.♗d3
♗d7 11.a3 0-0-0 12.0-0-0 ♘d4
13.♘d4 ♗d4 14.♗e3 ♗e3 15.fe3
♕g5 16.♕f2 ♗c6 17.♖hg1 ♕c5
18.♖ge1 ♗a4 19.♖d2 ♖d3 20.♖d3
♕c4 21.♖c3 ♕a2 22.♖c7 ♚c7
23.♕f4 ♚c8 24.♕a4 ♕a1 25.♚d2
♕b2 26.♕c2 ♕c2 27.♚c2 ♖g8
28.g3 ♖g4 29.♚d3 ♖a4 30.♖c1
♚d7 31.♖c3 f5 32.♚e2 h5 33.h4 b5
34.♚f3 ♚d6 35.♖c8 ♖a3 36.♖h8 b4
37.♖h5 b3 38.♖h8 ♖a6, 0-1

Game 32
Katalymov,B—Cherepkov,A
Lvov 1968

1.c4 ♘f6 2.♘c3 e6 3.e4 d5 4.e5 d4
5.ef6 dc3 6.fg7 cd2 7.♗d2 ♗g7
8.♕c2 ♘c6 9.♘f3 ♕e7 10.♗d3
♗d7 11.a3 0-0-0 12.♗g5 ♗f6 13.h4
h6 14.♗e3 ♗g7 15.0-0-0 f5
16.♖he1 ♖hf8 17.g3 e5 18.♘d2 e4
19.♗f1 ♘e5 20.♘b1 ♘f3 21.♖e2
♗c6 22.♘c3 ♖d1 23.♘d1 ♘d4
24.♗d4 ♗d4 25.♘e3 ♕e5 26.♗h3
♚b8 27.♕d2 ♗e3 28.♕e3 f4 29.gf4
♕f4 30.♖d2 ♕h4 31.b4 a6 32.♕c5
♕f6 33.b5 e3 34.♕e3 ab5 35.cb5
♗b5 36.♖d4 ♖e8 37.♕d2 ♕c6
38.♕c2 ♕h1, 0-1

English Opening [A27]

Game 33
Schweber,G—Anelli,A
Vilja 1971

1.c4 e5 2.♘c3 ♘c6 3.♘f3 f5 4.d4 e4
5.d5 ef3 6.dc6 fg2 7.cd7

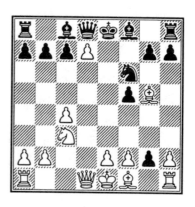

After 8.cd7

English Opening [A39]

Game 35
Saenz,D—Martinez,J
Canete 1994

1.c4 c5 2.♘f3 ♘f6 3.g3 g6 4.♗g2
♗g7 5.♘c3 ♘c6 6.0-0 0-0 7.d4 d5
8.cd5 cd4 9.dc6 dc3 10.cb7 cb2
11.ba8=♕ ba1=♕, 1/2-1/2

7...♕d7 8.♕d7 ♗d7 9.♗g2 0-0-0
10.♗f4 ♘f6 11.0-0-0 ♗c5 12.e3
♗e6 13.b3 c6 14.♗f3 ♖d1 15.♖d1
♖d8 16.♗e5 ♖d1 17.♔d1 = (...),
1/2-1/2

Game 34
Razuvaev,Y—Kupreichik,V
Dubna 1970

1.c4 e5 2.♘c3 ♘c6 3.♘f3 f5 4.d4
e4 5.♗g5 ♘f6 6.d5 ef3 7.dc6 fg2
8.cd7

(see next diagram)

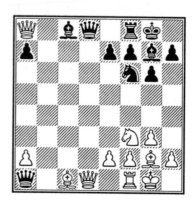

final position

8...♘d7! 9.♗d8 gh1=♕, 0-1

An effective opening trap!

Modern Defense
[A42]

Game 36
Agdestein,S—Keene,R
Gausdal 1983

1.d4 g6 2.c4 ♗g7 3.♘c3 d6 4.e4
♘c6 5.d5 ♘d4 6.♗e3 c5 7.♘ge2
♕b6 8.♘d4 cd4 9.♘a4 de3 10.♘b6
ef2

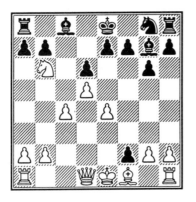

11.♔f2 ab6 12.♕c2 ♗d4 13.♔e1
♘f6 14.♗e2 0-0 15.♖d1 ♗e5 16.a4
h5 17.b3 ♗d7 18.♕d3 e6 19.de6
♗e6 20.♗f3 ♘d7 21.♔f2 b5 22.ab5
♖a2 23.♖d2 ♘c5 24.♕e3 ♖d2
25.♕d2 ♘b3 26.♕c2 ♗d4 27.♔g3
♗e5 28.♔f2 ♗d4 29.♔g3, 1/2-1/2

Dutch Defense
[A84]

Game 37
Shumjakina—Matveeva,S
Kstovo 1998

1.d4 e6 2.c4 b6 3.e4 ♗b7 4.♗d3 f5
5.ef5 ♗g2 6.♕h5 g6 7.fg6 ♗g7
8.gh7 ♔f8 (A typical feature of the
e4-f5-g6-h7 Steeplechase is the
pawn's support by a Bishop. The prel-
ate increases the strength of this tactical method)

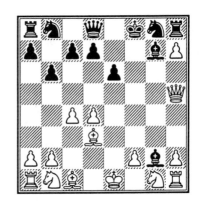

9.♗g5 ♘f6 10.♕h4 ♘c6 11.♘e2
♘b4 12.♗g6 ♗h1 13.♘bc3 ♗f3
14.♘f4 ♘c6 15.♗d3 ♔f7 16.♗g6
♔f8 17.♘e4 ♗e4 18.♗e4 ♘d4
19.0-0-0 c5 20.♘h5 ♖h7 21.♗f6
♗f6 22.♕f6 ♕f6 23.♘f6 ♖f7
24.♘d7 ♖d7 25.♗a8 ♘e2 26.♔c2
♘d4 27.♔c1 ♘e2 28.♔c2 ♘d4,
1/2-1/2

Owen's Defense
[B00]

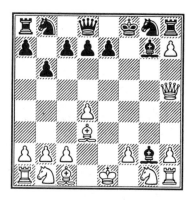

After 1.e4 b6 2.d4 ♗b7 3.♗d3 f5
4.ef5 ♗g2 5.♕h5 g6 6.fg6 ♗g7
7.gh7 ♔f8 (Completely analogous to
the previous game!)

Game 38
Zakeralo—Drevoricev
Yugoslavia 1965

1.e4 b6 2.d4 ♗b7 3.♗d3 f5 4.ef5
♗g2 5.♕h5 g6 6.fg6 ♗g7 7.gh7
♔f8 8.hg8=♕ ♔g8 9.♕g5 ♗h1
10.f3 ♖h2 11.♕d5 e6 12.♕a8 ♕h4
13.♔d1 ♕f2 14.♕b8 ♔f7 15.♘e2
♗f3 16.♘bc3 ♕f1 17.♔d2 ♗h6#,
0-1

Game 39
Shmit,A—Vitolins,A
USSR 1969

1.e4 b6 2.d4 ♗b7 3.♗d3 f5 (△ ×
♖h8) **4.ef5** (4.♕e2) **4...♗g2**
5.♕h5 g6 6.fg6 ♗g7 (6...♘f6??
7.gh7 ♘h5 8.♗g6#) **7.gh7 ♔f8**

8.hg8=♕ (8.♘e2!?) **8...♔g8**
(8...♖g8 9.♕f5 ♗f6 □ 10.♗h6 ♔f7
[10...♔e8 11.♕g6] 11.♕h5 ♔e6
12.♗f4, △ 13.♗f5) **9.♕g4 ♗h1**
10.h4 ♗d5! (10...e6 11.h5 ±)
11.h5 (△ 12.h6 →) **11...♗e6**
12.♕g2 (12.♕g6 ♗f7 13.♕g2 ♖h5
14.♕a8 ♗d5) **12...♖h5! 13.♕a8**
♗d5 14.♕a7 ♘c6 15.♕a4
(15.♕a6 ♖h1 16.♔f1 ♘d4)
15...♖h1 16.♔f1 ♘d4 17.♗c4
(△ 17.♘d2) **17...e6 18.♗d5 ed5**
19.♗f4 ♕h4 (19...♘f3) **20.♕a8**
♔h7 21.♕d5 ♕h3 (21...♖g1
22.♔g1 ♕f4 23.♕d7 [23.♘c3 ♕g4
24.♔f1 ♘c2 25.♕d3 +−] 23...♕c1
24.♔g2 ♕g5 25.♔h2 ♘f3 26.♔h3
♘g1 27.♔h2! =) **22.♕g2 ♖g1**
23.♔g1 ♘e2 24.♔f1 ♕g2
25.♔g2 ♘f4 26.♔f3 ♗b2
27.♔f4 ♗a1 28.c3 ♗b2 29.♔e3
♗c1, 1/2-1/2 (ChessBase)

Game 40
Bunjaev—Krivaus
corr. 1992

1.e4 b6 2.d4 ♗b7 3.♗d3 f5 4.ef5
♗g2 5.♕h5 g6 6.fg6 ♗g7 7.gh7
♔f8 8.♘f3 ♘f6 9.♕g6 ♗h1 10.♗h6
♘e8 11.♕f5 ♘f6 12.♗g7 ♔g7
13.♕g6 (13...♔f8 14.♕h6 ♔f7
15.♘g5 ♔e8 16.♗g6#), 1-0

Center Counter Defense [B01]

Game 41
Mieses,J—Ekvist
Nuremburg 1895

1.e4 d5 2.ed5 ♕d5 3.♘c3 ♕d8 4.d4 ♘c6 5.♘f3 ♗g4 6.d5 ♘e5

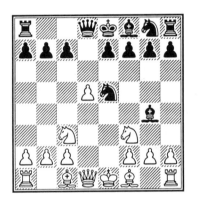

7.♘e5 (Black is caught in a typical trap. After 7...♗d1 8.♗b5 c6 9.dc6, White wins with a Steeplechase along either the d5-c6-b7 path or the d5-c6-c7 path), 1-0

Game 42
Federov—Cherny
Minsk 1988

1.e4 d5 2.ed5 ♘f6 3.♘c3 ♘d5 4.d4 ♘c3 5.bc3 ♘c6 6.♘f3 ♗g4 7.d5 ♘e5 8.♘e5 (Analogous to the preceding game) **8...♗d1 9.♗b5 c6 10.dc6 ♕d5?** (Correct was 10...♗e2 11.c7 ♗b5 12.cd8=♕ ♖d8) **11.cb7 ♔d8 12.♘c6 ♔d7**

13.ba8=♕ ♕b5 14.♔d1 ♕d5 15.♗d2 ♕g2 16.♕d8 ♔e6 17.♖e1, 1-0

Pirc Defense [B09]

Game 43
Byhovsky—Bebchuk,E
Moscow 1967

1.d4 ♘f6 2.♘c3 g6 3.e4 d6 4.f4 ♗g7 5.♘f3 0-0 6.e5 ♘fd7 7.h4 c5 8.h5 cd4 9.hg6 dc3 10.gf7 ♖f7 11.♘g5 cb2 (A mutual Steeplechase: h2-h4-h5-g6-f7 for White, and c7-c5-d4-c3-b2 for Black!)

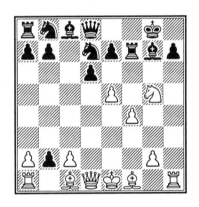

12.♗c4 ♘e5 13.♕h5 ♕a5 14.♔f1 d5 15.♗b2 ♖f4 16.♘f3 dc4 17.♗c1 ♖f6 18.♕h7 ♔f8 19.♗h6 ♗h6 20.♖h6 ♘f3 21.♖h5 ♘g5, 0-1

Caro-Kann Defense [B15]

Game 44
Schuster—Carls
Oldenburg 1913

**1.e4 c6 2.d4 d5 3.♞c3 de4
4.♞e4 ♞f6 5.♞g3 h5** (The pawn
starts on a long journey) **6.♗g5 h4
7.♗f6 hg3 8.♗e5 ♖h2** (Next
comes three intermediate moves.
Let's check our formula: 7 – 3 = 4.
Everything's all right!)

9.♖h2 ♛a5 10.c3 (10.♛d2 gf2)
10...♛e5 11.de5 gh2 (The appearance of a new Queen is inevita-
ble. Excelsior!), **0-1**

Caro-Kann Defense [B18]

Game 45
Davydov—Koshelev
USSR 1965

1.e4 c6 2.d4 d5 3.♞c3 de4 4.♞e4
♗f5 5.♞g3 ♗g6 6.♞h3 e6 7.♞f4

♗d6 8.h4 ♛c7 9.h5 ♗f4 10.hg6
♗g3 11.♖h7 (As in the previous
game, but with colors reversed)
11...♖h7 12.gh7

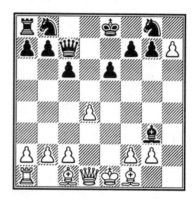

12...♛a5 13.c3 ♗f2 14.♔d2 ♗e3
15.♔c2, 1-0

Sicilian Defense [B23]

Game 46
Shchekachev—Vojzehorsky
Nizhny Novgorod 1998

1.e4 c5 2.♞c3 d6 3.f4 ♞c6 4.♞f3 g6
5.♗c4 ♗g7 6.0-0 ♞f6 7.d3 0-0
8.♛e1 ♞d4 9.♗b3 ♗e6 10.♞d4
cd4 (Starting a Steeplechase along
the main diagonal) 11.♗e6 dc3
12.♗b3 ♞e4 (An important intermediate move) 13.de4 cb2 (Black
emerges with an extra pawn)

(see next diagram)

14.♗b2 ♗b2 15.♖d1 a5 16.f5 ♔g7
17.♖f3 a4 18.♗c4 ♖c8 19.♗d3 ♗f6

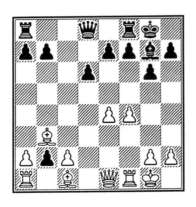

After 13...cb2

20.♔h1 ♖c5 21.♖h3 ♖h8 22.♖b1
♕c7 23.♕e2 ♖c8 24.♕e3 g5
25.♖g3 h6 26.h4 ♖h8 27.c4 ♔f8
28.hg5 hg5 29.♖h3 ♔g7 30.♖h8
♔h8 31.g3 ♖c6 32.♖b4 ♖a6
33.♔g2 ♔g7 34.♔f3 ♖a8 35.♔g2
♕c5 36.♕c5 dc5 37.♖b7 ♖d8
38.♗b1 g4 39.♔f2 ♖d2 40.♔f1
♗e5, 0-1

French Defense [C12]

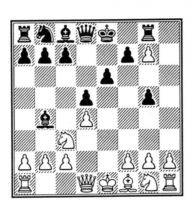

After 1.e4 e6 2.d4 d5 3.♘c3 ♘f6
4.♗g5 ♗b4 5.e5 h6 6.ef6 hg5 7.fg7
♖g8

Game 47
Tartakower,S—Vidmar,M
Vienna 1907

1.e4 e6 2.d4 d5 3.♘c3 ♘f6 4.♗g5
♗b4 5.e5 h6 6.ef6 hg5 7.fg7 ♖g8
8.h4 gh4 9.♕h5 ♖g7 10.♘f3 ♘d7
11.♖h4 ♘f6 12.♕h6 ♗f8 13.♕f4
♗d7 14.♘e5 ♕e7 15.♘d7 ♘d7
16.♘b5 e5 17.de5 ♘e5 18.0-0-0
0-0-0 19.♖h5 f6 20.♘a7 ♔b8
21.♘b5 ♕f7 22.♖f5 ♖g4 23.♕e5,
1-0

Game 48
Balla,Z—Brody,M
Budapest 1907

1.e4 e6 2.d4 d5 3.♘c3 ♘f6 4.♗g5
♗b4 5.e5 h6 6.ef6 hg5 7.fg7 ♖g8
8.♕h5 ♕f6 9.h4 ♕d4 10.♘ge2
♕g7 11.0-0-0 ♘d7 12.hg5 ♕g5
13.♕g5 ♖g5 14.♖h8 ♘f8 15.f4 ♖g4
16.♘b5 ♗a5 17.♘bd4 ♗d7 18.♘f3
0-0-0 19.♘e5 ♖g7 20.f5 ♘h7
21.♖d8 ♔d8 22.♘f4 ♔e7 23.♘d7
♔d7 24.♘d5 ef5 25.b4 ♗b4
26.♘b4 ♔c8 27.♗d3 ♖g5 28.g4 a5
29.♘d5, 1-0

Game 49
Forgacs,L—Spielmann,R
St. Petersburg 1912

1.e4 e6 2.d4 d5 3.♘c3 ♘f6 4.♗g5
♗b4 5.e5 h6 6.ef6 hg5 7.fg7 ♖g8
8.h4 gh4 9.♕h5 ♕f6 10.♘f3 ♘d7
11.0-0-0 ♗c3 12.bc3 ♕g7 13.♕h4
♘f8 14.♕f4 f6 15.♗d3 ♕e7 16.g3
c5 17.♖h6 c4 18.♗e2 ♘g6 19.♕g4
♕f7 20.♘h4 ♘h4 21.♕h4 ♔e7
22.f4 ♗d7 23.f5 ef5 24.♗c4 ♖g4
25.♖e1 ♗e6 26.♕h1 ♔d6 27.♖h7
♕g8 28.♗b3 ♖e4 29.♖b7 ♖c8
30.♕f1 ♖c6 31.♖e4, 1-0

Game 50
Grigoriev,N—Alekhine,A
Moscow 1915

1.e4 e6 2.d4 d5 3.♘c3 ♘f6 4.♗g5
♗b4 5.e5 h6 6.ef6 hg5 7.fg7 ♖g8
8.h4 gh4 9.♕g4 ♗e7 10.g3 c5
11.0-0-0 ♘c6 12.dc5 ♕a5 13.♔b1
e5 14.♕h5 ♗e6 15.♘d5 ♗d5
16.♖d5 ♘b4 17.♖e5 ♕a2 18.♔c1
0-0-0 19.♗d3 ♕a1 20.♔d2 ♕b2
21.♔e3 ♗f6 22.♕f5 ♔b8 23.♖e4
♖d3 24.cd3 ♗d4 25.♔f4 ♕f2, 0-1

Game 51
Tartakower,S—Wolf,S
Vienna 1923

1.e4 e6 2.d4 d5 3.♘c3 ♘f6 4.♗g5
♗b4 5.e5 h6 6.ef6 hg5 7.fg7 ♖g8
8.h4 gh4 9.♕h5 ♕f6 10.♘f3 ♘c6
11.♖h4 ♕g7 12.0-0-0 ♗d7 13.g3
0-0-0 14.♕h7 ♗e7 15.♖h5 ♗f6

16.♗b5 ♕h7 17.♖h7 ♖df8 18.♘e2
♖h8 19.♖dh1 a6 20.♗c6 ♗c6
21.♘e5 ♗e8 22.f4 ♖h7 23.♖h7
♖h8 24.♖h8 ♗h8 25.g4 f6 26.♘d3
b6 27.♔d2 ♔d7 28.b3 ♗g7 29.c4
dc4 30.bc4 ♗f8 31.♘c3 ♗g6 32.d5
ed5 33.♘d5 ♗g7 34.♔e3 ♔d6
35.f5 ♗f7 36.♔e4 ♗d5 37.cd5 ♗h6
38.♔d4 ♗g5 39.♘f2 c5 40.dc6 ♔c6
41.♘e4 ♗h4 42.♔e3 b5 43.♔d4 a5
44.a3 b4 45.ab4 ab4 46.♔c4 b3
47.♔b3 ♔d5 48.♘d2 ♔e5 49.♔c4
♔f4 50.♔d5 ♔g4 51.♔e6 ♔g5
52.♘f3, 1-0

Game 52
Belavenets,S—Bondarevsky,I
Tbilisi 1937

1.e4 e6 2.d4 d5 3.♘c3 ♘f6 4.♗g5
♗b4 5.e5 h6 6.ef6 hg5 7.fg7 ♖g8
8.h4 gh4 9.♕g4 ♕f6 10.♖h4 ♕g7
11.♕g7 ♖g7 12.♖h8 ♗f8 13.0-0-0
♗d7 14.♖e1 ♗c6 15.f4 ♘d7 16.f5
0-0-0 17.fe6 fe6 18.♖e6 ♖g4
19.♘f3 ♗g7 20.♖h5 ♘f6 21.♖f5
♘e4 22.♘e5 ♗e5 23.♖ee5 ♘g3
24.♗d3 ♖d4 25.♖f7 ♖h4 26.b3
♘e4 27.♗e4 de4 28.♖ee7 ♖e8
29.♖e8 ♗e8 30.♖f8 ♔d7 31.♔d2
♖g4 32.♖f2 ♔e6 33.♘e2, 1/2-1/2

Game 53
Krischewsky—Fu
Berlin 1961

**1.e4 e6 2.d4 d5 3.♘c3 ♘f6
4.♗g5 ♗b4 5.♗d3 c5 6.e5 cd4
7.ef6 dc3 8.fg7 cb2**

(The mutual Steeplechase has led to a very critical position) **9.♔f1 ♗c3!**
10.gh8=♕ ♗h8 11.♖b1
(11.♗d8 ba1=♕ 12.♕a1 ♗a1 –+)
11...♕g5 12.♘e2 ♘c6 13.c3
♗d7 14.♖b2? (△ 14.h4 ♕e7
15.♖b2) **14...d4 15.♖b7 dc3**
16.♗e4 ♕d2 –+ 17.♕a4 ♖c8
18.g3 ♘e5 19.♕a6 f5 20.♖d7
♔d7 21.♕a4 ♔e7 22.♕a7 ♘d7
23.♕a6 ♖b8 24.♘f4♕d6
25.♕d6 ♔d6, 0-1

Center Opening [C20]

1.e4 e5 2.c3 ♘c6 3.d4 ♘f6
4.♗g5 h6 5.♗h4 g5 6.♗g3 ed4
7.e5 dc3 8.ef6 cb2 9.♕e2 ♕e7!!
(A fantastic move! This mutual Steeplechase [e5-d4-c3-b2 and e5-f6-e7] ends in immediate victory for Black) **10.fe7 ♗g7!, 0-1**

final position

Game 55
Saullson—Filips
Chicago 1907

1.d4 ♘c6 2.e4 e5 3.d5 ♘ce7 4.f4 d6
5.♘f3 ♗g4 6.♘c3 ♘g6 7.h3 ♗f3
8.♗b5 c6 9.dc6 ♗d1 10.cb7 ♔e7
11.♘d5 ♔e6 12.f5#, 1-0

Danish Gambit [C21]

After 1.e4 e5 2.d4 ed4 3.c3 dc3
4.♗c4 cb2 5.♗b2

A rare case, in which the e7-e5-d4-c3-b2 Steeplechase begins on the first move. This gambit contains a quite sensible idea. Sacrificing two pawns, White places both Bishops on ideal squares. Practice shows that it's dangerous to accept all the sacrifices, seeing that White leaves his opponent far behind in development and launches a strong attack. The greatest follower of the Danish Gambit at the beginning of our century was Grandmaster Jacob Mieses.

Nevertheless, the age of dashing attacks has passed and the opening is almost never used nowadays. As A.Alehkine has shown, the main reason for its lack of popularity is that Black, by means of 5...d5 6.♗d5 ♘f6 7.♗f7 ♔f7 8.♕d8 ♗b4, can pass on to an equal ending. The world champion managed to find a method of strengthening White's play – one's ambition must be limited to the sacrifice of only a single pawn, by playing 4.♘c3 instead of 4.♗c4.

Game 56
Linden—Machusky
Paris 1863

1.e4 e5 2.d4 ed4 3.c3 dc3 4.♗c4 cb2 5.♗b2 ♗b4 6.♘c3 ♘f6 7.♘ge2 ♘e4 8.0-0 ♘c3 9.♘c3 ♗c3 10.♗c3 ♕g5 11.♖e1 ♔d8 12.f4 ♕f4 13.♗g7 ♖g8 14.♕g4 ♕d6 15.♗f6, 1-0

Game 57
Charousek,R—Brosztel
Kassa 1893

1.e4 e5 2.d4 ed4 3.c3 dc3 4.♗c4 cb2 5.♗b2 ♗b4 6.♘c3 d6 7.♘f3 ♗g4 8.♕b3 ♗c3 9.♗c3 ♔f8 10.♗f7 ♘f6 11.♘d4 ♘e4 12.♗h5 ♕e7 13.♗g4 ♘c5 14.♘e6 ♔e8 15.♕b5 c6 16.♕e2 ♘e6 17.♕e6 h5 18.♗f5 ♖f8 19.0-0 ♘d7 20.♗g6 ♔d8 21.♕e7 ♔e7 22.♖ae1 ♔d8 23.♗g7 ♖g8 24.♗h5, 1-0

Game 58
Dorrer—Bilenkin
St. Petersburg 1897

1.e4 e5 2.d4 ed4 3.c3 dc3 4.♗c4 cb2 5.♗b2 ♘h6 6.♘c3 ♗b4 7.♘f3 0-0 8.♕c2 d6 9.0-0-0 ♗e6 10.♘d5 ♗a5 11.h4 ♘d7 12.♘g5 c6 13.♘e3 ♗c4 14.e5 g6 15.♘c4 d5 16.♘d6 ♗c7 17.♕c3 ♘f6 18.♘b7 ♕b8 19.♘c5 ♖e8 20.e6 ♗d8 21.g3 ♕b5 22.♘d7 ♕c4 23.♕c4 dc4 24.♘f6 ♗f6 25.♗f6 fe6 26.♖d7 ♘g4 27.♖g7, 1-0

Game 59
Tenunovic—Zanibelli
Sabadka 1897

1.e4 e5 2.d4 ed4 3.c3 dc3 4.♗c4 cb2 5.♗b2 ♘f6 6.♘f3 ♘e4 7.0-0 ♘f6 8.♖e1 ♗e7 9.♗f6 gf6 10.♕d5 ♖f8 11.♘c3 d6 12.♘e4 ♗e6 13.♘d4 c6 14.♕h5 ♔d7 15.♗e6 fe6 16.♘e6 ♕e8 17.♕h3 f5 18.♘f8

♕f8 19.♘g3 ♘a6 20.♘f5 ♗f6
21.♘d4, 1-0

Game 60
Soldatenkov,K—Durnovo
St. Petersburg 1898

1.e4 e5 2.d4 ed4 3.c3 dc3 4.♗c4
cb2 5.♗b2 ♘f6 6.e5 ♗b4 7.♘c3
♕e7 8.♘ge2 ♘e4 9.0-0 ♘c3
10.♗c3 ♗c3 11.♘c3 0-0 12.♘d5
♕e5 13.♖e1 ♕d6 14.♕h5 c6
15.♘c7 g6 16.♕h6 ♕c7 17.♗f7
♔f7 18.♕h7 ♔f6 19.♕h4 ♔g7
20.♖e7 ♖f7 21.♕d4 ♔f8 22.♕h8
♔e7 23.♖e1 ♔d6 24.♕d4#, 1-0

Game 61
Mieses,J—Chigorin,M
Hannover 1902

1.e4 e5 2.d4 ed4 3.c3 dc3 4.♗c4
cb2 5.♗b2 ♕e7 6.♘c3 c6 7.♕c2 d6
8.0-0-0 ♗e6 9.♗e2 ♘d7 10.♘f3
♘c5 11.♖d4 0-0-0 12.♖hd1 ♕c7
13.♘a4 ♘d7 14.♖1d3 ♘gf6 15.♖c3
♗e7 16.♖b4 ♘b8 17.♘d4 d5
18.♘c6 ♘c6 19.♗a6 ♕f4 20.♖e3
♗b4 21.♕c6 ♕c7 22.♗b7 ♔b8
23.♗e5 ♕e5 24.♖b3 ♕c7, 0-1

Game 62
Rabinovich,A—Chigorin,M
Kiev 1903

1.e4 e5 2.d4 ed4 3.c3 dc3 4.♗c4
cb2 5.♗b2 ♕e7 6.♘d2 ♘f6 7.♘gf3
d5 8.♗f6 gf6 9.♗d5 c6 10.♗c4 ♖g8
11.0-0 ♗h3 12.♘h4 ♘d7 13.♕h5

♘e5 14.♖fc1 0-0-0 15.♘f5 ♗f5
16.♕f5 ♕d7 17.♕d7 ♖d7 18.♘b3
♖g4 19.♗f1 ♖e4 20.♖ab1 ♖b4
21.g3 ♔c7 22.♖d1 ♖d1 23.♖d1
♖a4 24.♘d4 ♖d4, 0-1

Game 63
Mieses,J—Maroczy,G
Monte Carlo 1903

1.e4 e5 2.d4 ed4 3.c3 dc3 4.♗c4
cb2 5.♗b2 d6 6.♘e2 ♘c6 7.0-0
♗e6 8.♗d5 ♘f6 9.♕b3 ♕c8
10.♘f4 ♗d5 11.ed5 ♘e5 12.♖e1
♗e7 13.♗e5 de5 14.♖e5 ♕d7
15.♕g3 0-0-0 16.♕g7 ♕d6 17.♕g5
♖he8 18.♘d2 ♘d7 19.♖e7 ♕e7
20.♕g3 ♕b4 21.♘f3 ♖g8 22.♕h4
♕c3 23.♖b1 ♕f3 24.♕h6 ♘b6, 0-1

Game 64
Mieses,J—Chigorin,M
Cambridge Springs 1904

1.e4 e5 2.d4 ed4 3.c3 dc3 4.♗c4
cb2 5.♗b2 ♕e7 6.♘c3 c6 7.♘ge2
b5 8.♗b3 a5 9.♖c1 ♘a6 10.0-0
♘c5 11.♘d4 ♘b3 12.♘f5 ♕e6
13.ab3 ♘f6 14.♘e2 ♘h5 15.f4 ♕g6
16.♘ed4 ♘f6 17.♕c2 ♗b7 18.♘b5
cb5 19.♕c7 ♗b4 20.♕b7 0-0
21.♖f3 ♖ab8 22.♕a7 ♘e4 23.♘g3
♘d2 24.♖e3 ♖bc8 25.♖c8 ♖c8
26.♕d7 ♕b1 27.♔f2 ♕c2 28.♘e2
♖f8 29.♕d4 f6 30.g4 ♔h8 31.♔g2
♘b3 32.♕d3 ♕b2 33.♕b3 ♕b3
34.♖b3 ♖c8 35.♘d4 ♖c4 36.♖d3
♔g8 37.f5 ♔f7 38.h3 ♖c5 39.♘e6
♖c2 40.♔f1 ♔e7 41.♖d5 g6 42.♖b5

gf5 43.gf5 ♔d6 44.♘d4 ♖c4
45.♘b3 ♔c6 46.♖b8 a4 47.♖c8
♔d5 48.♖d8 ♔e5 49.♘d2 ♗d2
50.♖d2 ♔f5 51.♖d5 ♔e4 52.♖a5
♔d3 53.♖a7 ♔c3 54.♖h7 a3, 1-0

Game 65
Janowsky,D—Marshall,F
Paris 1907

1.e4 e5 2.d4 ed4 3.c3 dc3 4.♗c4
cb2 5.♗b2 ♘f6 6.♘f3 d5 7.ed5
♗b4 8.♘c3 ♕e7 9.♗e2 ♘e4
10.♖c1 0-0 11.0-0 ♘c3 12.♖c3
♗c3 13.♗c3 ♘d7 14.♖e1 ♘f6
15.♗d3 ♕d8 16.♖e5 ♖e8 17.♖g5
h6 18.♖g3 ♘h5 19.♗c2 ♘g3
20.hg3 f5 21.g4 ♖e4 22.♘e5 ♕g5
23.d6 cd6 24.♕d6 ♕c1 25.♗d1
♖e5 26.♗e5 ♔h7 27.♔h2 ♗e6
(28.♕e7 ♖g8 29.♕e6 ♕d1 30.♕f5
♔h8 31.♕g6 ♕c1 [31...♕d2? 32.f4
33.♕h6#] 32.♗g7 ♖g7 33.♕e8 =),
1/2-1/2

Game 66
Marshall,F—Duras,O
New York 1913

1.e4 e5 2.d4 ed4 3.c3 dc3 4.♗c4
cb2 5.♗b2 ♘f6 6.e5 d5 7.ef6 dc4
8.♕d8 ♔d8 9.fg7 ♗b4 10.♘c3 ♖e8
11.♘ge2 ♗f5 12.0-0-0 ♘d7
13.♘d5 ♗d6 14.♗f6 ♘f6 15.♘f6
♔e7 16.♘e8 ♖e8 17.♖d4 ♔f6
18.♘g3 ♗a3 19.♔d1 ♗g6 20.f4
♗d3 21.♘h5 ♔g6 22.♖e1 ♖g8
23.♖d5 h6 24.♖e3 ♗b2 25.g4 ♗g7

26.f5 ♔h7 27.♖e7 ♖f8 28.♖c7 ♗c3
29.♖d3 ♗e5 30.♖c4, 1-0

Game 67
Nyholm,G—Reti,R
Baden Baden 1914

1.e4 e5 2.d4 ed4 3.c3 dc3 4.♗c4 d5
5.♗d5 cb2 6.♗b2 ♘f6 7.♘f3 ♗b4
8.♔f1 0-0 9.♕b3 ♘c6 10.♘c3 ♕e7
11.a3 ♗d6 12.♖e1 ♘e5 13.♘e5
♗e5 14.♗c4 c6 15.h4 b5 16.♗e2
♗e6 17.♕c2 ♕c5 18.♖c1 ♖fd8
19.g3 a5 20.♕b1 ♖d2 21.♘d5 ♖b2
22.♕b2 ♕d5 23.ed5 ♗b2 24.♖c2
♗d5, 0-1

Game 68
Nyholm,G—Tartakower,S
Baden Baden 1914

1.e4 e5 2.d4 ed4 3.c3 dc3 4.♗c4 d5
5.♗d5 cb2 6.♗b2 ♘f6 7.♗f7 ♔f7
8.♕d8 ♗b4 9.♕d2 ♗d2 10.♘d2
♖e8 11.f3 ♘c6 12.♖c1 ♗e6 13.a3
♖ad8 14.♘e2 ♖e7 15.♘c4 ♗c4
16.♖c4 ♘d7 17.♘d4 ♘d4 18.♖d4
c5 19.♖d5 ♖c8 20.♔e2 ♖c6 21.♖c1
g6 22.g4 a6 23.h4 b5 24.h5 c4
25.hg6 hg6 26.♗c3 ♘b6 27.♖d8
♖d7 28.♖d7 ♘d7 29.♖d1 ♘c5
30.♖d5 ♘a4 31.♔d2 ♘c3 32.♔c3
♖f6 33.♔d4 ♖f3 34.♔e5 ♖a3
35.♖d7 ♔e8 36.♖a7 ♔d8 37.g5
♖a1 38.♔d6 ♖d1 39.♔e6 c3, 0-1

Game 69
Marshall,F—Molotkovsky
USA 1914

1.e4 e5 2.d4 ed4 3.c3 dc3 4.♗c4
cb2 5.♗b2 d5 6.♗d5 ♗b4 7.♔f1
♘f6 8.♕b3 ♕e7 9.♘f3 ♘c6 10.a3
♗c5 11.♘bd2 0-0 12.♖c1 ♗g4
13.♗c6 bc6 14.♘e5 ♖ad8 15.♘dc4
♘e4 16.♘g4 ♘d2 17.♘d2 ♖d2
18.♘h6 ♔h8 19.♗g7 ♔g7 20.♘f5,
1-0

Game 70
Stolberg,M—Golovko,N
USSR 1939

1.e4 e5 2.d4 ed4 3.c3 dc3 4.♗c4
cb2 5.♗b2 d5 6.ed5 ♘f6 7.♘f3
♗b4 8.♘bd2 0-0 9.0-0 b5 10.♗d3
♕d5 11.♕b1 ♗b7 12.♗f6 ♗d2
13.♗h7 ♔h8 14.♗b2 ♗f4 15.♖d1
♗h2 16.♔h2 ♕h5 17.♔g3 f5
18.♗f5 ♕f5 19.♕f5, 1-0

Game 71
Kotrc,J—Petrovic
Yugoslavia 1970

1.e4 e5 2.d4 ed4 3.c3 dc3 4.♗c4
cb2 5.♗b2 d5 6.♗d5 ♘f6 7.♘c3
♘d5 8.♘d5 ♘c6 9.♘f3 ♗g4 10.h3
♗h5 11.0-0 ♕d7 12.♖b1 0-0-0
13.♕b3 ♗f3 14.♗g7 ♘a5 15.♕e3
♖g8 16.♕a7 ♕h3 17.♘b6 cb6
18.♖fc1 ♘c6 19.gh3 ♖g7 20.♔f1
♖d1 21.♖d1 ♘a7, 0-1

Game 72
Mieses,J—Finn
New York 1903

1.e4 e5 2.d4 ed4 3.c3 dc3 4.♗c4 c2
5.♕c2 ♘c6 6.♘c3 ♘f6 7.♘f3 d6
8.♗g5 ♗e7 9.0-0-0 ♗g4 10.e5 ♗f3
11.ef6 gf6 12.gf3 fg5 13.♕f5 ♘e5
14.♖he1 ♘c4 15.♘d5 ♘e5 16.♖e5
de5 17.♕e5 f6 18.♘c7 ♔f8 19.♘e6
♔g8 20.♖d8 ♖d8 21.♕c7 ♖e8
22.♕c4 b5 23.♕d5 ♖f8 24.♘g5
♔g7 25.♘e6 ♔g6 26.♘f8 ♖f8
27.♕b5 f5 28.♕d7 ♗g5 29.♔c2
♖d8 30.♕a7 ♖d2 31.♔c3 ♖e2
32.b4 ♗f6 33.♔d3 ♖b2 34.♔c4
♖c2 35.♔b5, 1-0

An original interpretation of the
Danish Gambit was seen in the next
game. With 3...d5, Rubinstein de-
nied his opponent's Bishop access to
the c4-square, and White couldn't
get compensation for the sacrificed
pawn. Later Mieses found the
strengthening 4.ed5.

Game 73
Mieses,J—Rubinstein,A
Prague 1908

1.e4 e5 2.d4 ed4 3.c3 d5 4.e5 dc3
5.♘f3 cb2 6.♗b2 ♘h6 7.♘c3 ♗e6
8.♗d3 ♗e7 9.♕c2 ♘c6 10.a3 ♕d7
11.♗c1 ♘f5 12.♕a4 0-0 13.♕f4 f6
14.g4 fe5 15.♘e5 ♘e5 16.♕e5
♗f6, 0-1

Vienna Game [C27]

Game 74
Tartakower,S—Spielmann,R
Ostende 1907

1.e4 e5 2.♘c3 ♘f6 3.♗c4 ♘e4
4.♕h5 ♘d6 5.♗b3 ♘c6 6.♘b5 g6
7.♕f3 ♘f5 8.g4 a6 9.gf5 ab5 10.fg6
♕e7 11.gf7 (Excelsior! [Nearly.
V.Ch.] This pawn's destiny will define the game's destiny. Tartakower)

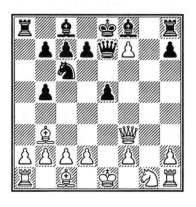

11...♔d8 12.d3 ♘d4 13.♕h5 ♗g7
14.♘f3 ♖a6 15.♘d4 ed4 16.♔f1
♖g6 17.♗d2 d6 18.♖e1 ♗g4
19.♖e7 ♗h5 20.♖e1 ♗f3 21.♖g1
♗e5 22.♗h6 ♔e7 23.♗g7 ♖d8
24.♗e5 de5 25.♖e5 ♔f8 26.♖g3
♗c6 27.♖eg5 ♖dd6 28.♖h5 ♖g3
29.hg3 h6 30.g4 ♗f3 31.♖b5 b6
32.♖e5 ♖d8 33.g5 h5 34.g6, 1-0

Game 75
Book,E—Hildenhejmo
Helsinki 1924

1.e4 e5 2.♘c3 ♘f6 3.♗c4 ♘e4
4.♕h5 ♘g5 5.d4 ♘e6 6.d5 g6 7.de6
gh5 8.ef7 ♔e7 (Now begins the
pursuit of Black's King, which will
end in mate)

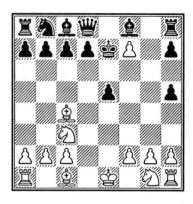

9.♗g5 ♔d6 10.0-0-0 ♔c5 11.♖d5
♔c4 12.b3 ♔b4 13.♖b5 ♔a3
14.♘b1 ♔a2 15.♖a5 ♗a3
16.♖a3#, 1-0

King's Gambit [C35]

The Cunningham gambit embodies
an idea that is familiar to us. The
name must be a mistake, because the
Italian Greco analyzed this gambit
100 years before the Scottish
chessplayer was born! Here the Steeplechase is "traded" for an advantage
in development. White sacrifices
three pawns in turn along the
e5-f4-g3-h2 route, and the resulting

Black h2-pawn is used as shelter for the White King.

The gambit is rarely used now – in his *Analyses* Philidor had already proven it's inefficiency. Although the Cunningham has virtually disappeared from modern practice, it remains a monument to masters of the past.

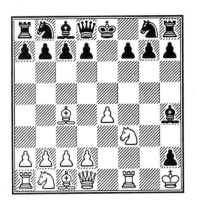

After 1.e4 e5 2.f4 ef4 3.♘f3 ♗e7 4.♗c4 ♗h4 5.g3 fg3 6.0-0 gh2 7.♔h1

Game 76
N.N.—Philidor,A
London 1790

1.e4 e5 2.f4 ef4 3.♘f3 ♗e7 4.♗c4 ♗h4 5.g3 fg3 6.0-0 gh2 7.♔h1 ♗f6 8.e5 d5 9.ef6 ♘f6 10.♗b3 ♗e6 11.d3 h6 12.♗f4 c5 13.♗h2 ♘c6 14.♘bd2 ♘g4 15.♕e2 ♘h2 16.♕h2 ♕b8 17.♕b8 ♖b8 18.♖ae1 ♔d7 19.♘e5 ♘e5 20.♖e5 ♔d6 21.♖fe1 b5 22.c3 ♖be8 23.a4 a6 24.♘f3 g5 25.♔g2 f6 26.♖5e2 h5

27.ab5 ab5 28.♖a1 ♖a8 29.♖ae1 ♗d7 30.d4 c4 31.♗c2 h4 32.♖h1 ♖h5 33.b3 ♖ah8 34.b4 g4 35.♘d2 ♖g5 36.♖f1 g3 37.♖f6 ♔c7 38.♖g6 h3 39.♔g1 g2 40.♖g5 h2 41.♔g2 h1=♕ 42.♔f2 ♖f8 43.♔e3 ♕h3 44.♘f3 ♕f3, 0-1

Game 77
Guttzeit—Kiezeritzky,L
Dorpt 1832

1.e4 e5 2.f4 ef4 3.♘f3 ♗e7 4.♗c4 ♗h4 5.g3 fg3 6.0-0 gh2 7.♔h1 ♗f6 8.e5 d5 9.ef6 ♘f6 10.♗b3 ♗e6 11.d4 ♘e4 12.♗f4 f5 13.♘bd2 0-0 14.c4 c6 15.♖c1 ♘d7 16.cd5 cd5 17.♘e4 fe4 18.♘g5 ♕e7 19.♕h5 ♘f6 20.♕h2 ♖ad8 21.♗c7 ♖d7 22.♗a4 h6 23.♘e6 ♕e6 24.♗d7 ♕d7 25.♗e5, 1-0

Game 78
Bilguer,P—Majet
Berlin 1838

1.e4 e5 2.f4 ef4 3.♘f3 ♗e7 4.♗c4 ♗h4 5.g3 fg3 6.0-0 gh2 7.♔h1 d6 8.♗f7 ♔f7 9.♘h4 ♘f6 10.d4 ♗h3 11.♖f3 ♗g4 12.♖f6 ♕f6 13.♕g4 ♕f1 14.♔h2 ♕c1 15.♘c3 ♕a1 16.♕f5 ♔e8 17.♕c8 ♔f7 18.♕c7 ♔e8 19.♕c8 ♔f7 20.♕b7 ♔e8 21.♘f5, 1-0

Game 79
Lazard,F—Jaenisch,C
Berlin 1842

1.e4 e5 2.f4 ef4 3.♘f3 ♗e7 4.♗c4 ♗h4 5.g3 fg3 6.0-0 gh2 7.♔h1 ♗f6 8.♘e5 ♗e5 9.♕h5 ♕e7 10.♖f7 ♕c5 11.♖f8 ♔e7 12.d4 ♕c4 13.♕e8 ♔d6 14.♕e5 ♔c6 15.♘a3 d6 16.d5 ♔c5 17.♗e3 ♔b4 18.c3 ♔a4 19.b3 ♔a3 20.♗c1 #, 1-0

Game 80
Jaenisch,C—Lazard,F
Berlin 1842

1.e4 e5 2.f4 ef4 3.♘f3 ♗e7 4.♗c4 ♗h4 5.g3 fg3 6.0-0 gh2 7.♔h1 ♗f6 8.♘e5 ♕e7 9.♗f7 ♔d8 10.d4 ♗e5 11.de5 ♕e5 12.♘c3 ♘f6 13.♗f4 ♕e7 14.e5 ♕f7 15.ef6 gf6 16.♗e5 ♖f8 17.♖f6 ♕g7 18.♗c7 ♔e8 19.♕e2 ♕e7 20.♖e1 ♘c6 21.♕h5 ♖f7 22.♕f7 #, 1-0

Game 81
Morphy,P—Bird,H
London 1859

1.e4 e5 2.f4 ef4 3.♘f3 ♗e7 4.♗c4 ♗h4 5.g3 fg3 6.0-0 gh2 7.♔h1 d5 8.♗d5 ♘f6 9.♗f7 ♔f7 10.♘h4 ♖e8 11.d3 ♗h3 12.♕h5 ♔g8 13.♖f6 gf6 14.♘c3 ♖e5 15.♕f3 ♕d7 16.♗f4 ♘c6 17.♔h2 ♗g4 18.♖g1 h5 19.♗e5 fe5 20.♘d5 ♘d4 21.♘f6 ♔h8 22.♕e3 ♕g7 23.♘h5 ♕h7 24.♖g4 ♕h5 25.♕h3 ♔h7 26.c3 ♘e6 27.♖g6 ♖e8 28.♖e6 ♖e6

29.♕e6 ♕h4 30.♕h3 ♕h3 31.♔h3 c5 32.♔g4 ♔g6 33.♔f3 ♔f6 34.♔e3 ♔e6 35.d4 ed4 36.cd4 cd4 37.♔d4 ♔d6 38.e5 ♔e6 39.♔e4 ♔e7 40.♔d5 ♔d7 41.e6 ♔e7 42.♔e5 a6 43.a3 ♔e8 44.♔d6 ♔d8 45.e7 ♔e8, 1-0

Game 82
Dus-Chotimirsky,F—Rabine
1910

1.e4 e5 2.f4 ef4 3.♘f3 ♗e7 4.♗c4 ♗h4 5.g3 fg3 6.0-0 gh2 7.♔h1 d5 8.ed5 ♗f6 9.d4 ♘e7 10.♘g5 h6 11.♘f7 ♔f7 12.d6 ♔f8 13.♕h5 ♕e8 14.♖f6 gf6 15.♕h6 ♖h6 16.♗h6 #, 1-0

Game 83
Helabert—Bermudez,S
Cuba 1923

1.e4 e5 2.f4 ef4 3.♘f3 ♗e7 4.♗c4 ♗h4 5.g3 fg3 6.0-0 gh2 7.♔h1 ♗e7 8.♗f7 ♔f7 9.♘e5 ♔e8 10.♕h5 g6 11.♘g6 ♘f6 12.♖f6 ♗f6 13.♘e5 ♔e7 14.♕f7 ♔d6 15.♘c4 ♔c5 16.♕d5 ♔b4 17.a3 ♔a4 18.b3 #, 1-0

Scotch Gambit [C44]

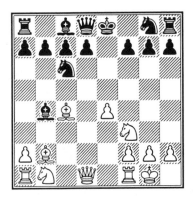

After 1.e4 e5 2.♘f3 ♘c6 3.d4 ed4 4.♗c4 ♗b4 5.c3 dc3 6.0-0 cb2 7.♗b2

It is clear that this attempt is a brother of the Danish gambit. Comparing the two openings, we find that two additional moves (♘f3 and 0-0 for White; ...♘c6 and ...♗b4 for Black) are present in the Scotch gambit. Black's wayward ♗b4 seems absolutely useless, and only supports the White attack.

Game 84
Bilguer,P—Lazard,F
Berlin 1839

1.e4 e5 2.♘f3 ♘c6 3.d4 ed4 4.♗c4 ♗b4 5.c3 dc3 6.0-0 cb2 7.♗b2 f6 8.♕b3 ♘h6 9.e5 fe5 10.♘e5 ♕e7 11.♘c6 bc6 12.♗g7 ♕g7 13.♕b4 d5 14.♖e1 ♔d8 15.♘c3 ♗h3 16.g3 dc4 17.♖ad1 ♗d7 18.♕b7 ♖c8 19.♕c6 ♖e8 20.♖d7 ♕d7 21.♕f6

♖e7 22.♘d5 ♘g8 23.♕g5 ♕e8 24.♖d1, 1-0

Game 85
Bilguer,P—Majet
Vienna 1839

1.e4 e5 2.♘f3 ♘c6 3.d4 ed4 4.♗c4 ♗b4 5.c3 dc3 6.0-0 cb2 7.♗b2 f6 8.♕b3 ♔f8 9.e5 fe5 10.♗e5 ♗e7 11.♗c3 d6 12.♘bd2 ♗f6 13.♗g8 ♖g8 14.♘e4 ♗c3 15.♘eg5 ♕e8 16.♘h7 ♔e7 17.♕c3 ♖g6 18.♖fe1 ♔d8 19.♘hg5 ♗f5 20.♕b3 ♔d7 21.♖ac1 ♖ab8 22.♘h4 ♕g5 23.♕f7 ♘e7 24.♘f5 ♖ge8 25.♘e7 ♕f6 26.♖c7 ♔c7 27.♘d5 ♔c6 28.♖c1 ♔b5 29.♕d7 ♔a6 30.♘f6, 1-0

Game 86
Witkomb—Kiezeritzky,L
Paris 1845

1.e4 e5 2.♘f3 ♘c6 3.d4 ed4 4.♗c4 ♗b4 5.c3 dc3 6.0-0 cb2 7.♗b2 ♔f8 8.♕d5 ♕e7 9.♘g5 ♘d8 10.a3 c6 11.♕d4 ♕g5 12.ab4 ♘e6 13.♕d6 ♕e7 14.♕d2 ♘f6 15.♗a3 b5 16.e5 ♘e4 17.♕d3 d5 18.♗d5 cd5 19.♕d5 ♗b7 20.♕b5 h5 21.♕d3 ♕g5 22.b5 ♔g8 23.f3 ♖d8 24.♗d6 ♘f4 25.♕c2 ♖c8 26.♕b2 ♘d3 27.♕e2 ♘c1 28.♕b2 ♕e3 29.♔h1 ♘d3 30.♖a3 ♘df2 31.♔g1 ♘h3 32.♔h1 ♕g1 33.♖g1 ♘hf2 34.♕f2 ♘f2#, 0-1

Game 87
Morphy, P—Sharpautje
New Orleans 1849

1.e4 e5 2.♘f3 ♘c6 3.d4 ed4 4.♗c4
♗b4 5.c3 dc3 6.0-0 cb2 7.♗b2 ♗f8
8.e5 d6 9.♖e1 de5 10.♘e5 ♕d1
11.♗f7 ♔e7 12.♘g6 ♔f7 13.♘h8 #,
1-0

final position

Game 88
Reshevsky, S—Gollney
Grand Rapids 1921

1.e4 e5 2.♘f3 ♘c6 3.d4 ed4 4.♗c4
♗b4 5.c3 dc3 6.0-0 cb2 7.♗b2 f6
8.e5 d5 9.♗d5 ♗g4 10.ef6 ♘f6
11.♗c6 bc6 12.♕b3 ♗f3 13.♕f3
♕d5 14.♕e2 ♔f7 15.♘c3 ♗c3
16.♗c3 ♖he8 17.♕c2 ♖e6 18.♖ad1
♕c5 19.♕d3 ♖d6 20.♕f3 ♕h5
21.♖d6 ♕f3 22.♖f6 ♕f6 23.♗f6
♔f6 24.♖c1 ♖d8 25.♖c6 ♖d6
26.♖c1 ♔e6 27.♔f1 ♔d7 28.♔e2
♖a6 29.♖c2 c5 30.♖c5 ♖a2 31.♔e3
♔d6 32.♖b5 ♖a3 33.♔f4 ♖c3 34.h4

♖c7 35.g4 ♔c6 36.♖b1 ♖f7 37.♔g3
a5 38.f4 a4 39.f5 ♖b7 40.♖c1 ♔b5
41.g5 a3 42.♔f4 ♔a4 43.f6 a2
44.♖a1 ♔b3 45.♔e5 ♔b2 46.♖a2
♔a2 47.♔e6 ♔b3 48.f7 ♖b6 (...), 1-0

The Modern Move Order

This variation strengthens Black's
play, but does not give him full
equality.

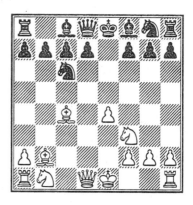

After 1.e4 e5 2.♘f3 ♘c6 3.d4 ed4
4.c3 dc3 5.♗c4 cb2 6.♗b2

Game 89
Klovan—Suetin, A
Minsk 1962

1.e4 e5 2.♘f3 ♘c6 3.d4 ed4 4.c3
dc3 5.♗c4 cb2 6.♗b2 ♗b4 7.♘c3
♘f6 8.♕c2 d6 9.0-0-0 0-0 10.e5
♘g4 11.h4 ♘ce5 12.♘d5 ♗c5
13.♘g5 g6 14.♘e4 ♗f5 15.f4 c6
16.fe5 cd5 17.♗d5 ♖c8 18.♔b1
♘e3 19.♕e2 ♕b6 20.♔a1 ♗e4

21.♗e4 ♘d1 22.♖d1 de5 23.♗e5
♖fe8 24.♗b2 ♖cd8 25.♖d8 ♖d8,
0-1

Game 90
Marjasin—Epstein
Bobrujsk 1967

1.e4 e5 2.♘f3 ♘c6 3.d4 ed4 4.c3
dc3 5.♗c4 cb2 6.♗b2 d5 7.♗d5
♘f6 8.0-0 ♗e7 9.♕b3 0-0 10.♖d1
♕e8 11.♘a3 a6 12.♖ac1 ♗d8
13.♘c4 ♘e7 14.♗f7 ♖f7 15.♘ce5
♘c6 16.♖c6 bc6 17.♘g5 ♗e7
18.♘ef7 ♔f8 19.e5 ♘d5 20.♕f3
♔g8 21.♖d5 ♗g4 22.♕e4 ♗g5
23.♘g5 ♕h5 24.♖d4, 1-0

Game 91
Ljubojevic,L—Kovac
Sarajevo 1970

1.e4 e5 2.♘f3 ♘c6 3.d4 ed4 4.c3
dc3 5.♗c4 cb2 6.♗b2 d6 7.♘c3
♗e6 8.♘d5 ♕d7 9.♖c1 ♘ge7
10.0-0 ♘g6 11.♕a4 a6 12.♖fe1 ♖a7
13.♗f1 ♔d8 14.♕b3 b6 15.♕e3
♘ge7 16.♖ed1 f6 17.♗c4 ♗d5
18.♗d5 ♘d5 19.ed5 ♘e7 20.♘d4
♔e8 21.♕f3 ♔f7 22.♖e1 ♖a8
23.♖e6 h5 24.♖ce1 ♖c8 25.♘c6
♘c6 26.♖f6 ♔g8 27.dc6 ♕g4
28.♕d5 ♔h7 29.♖f5 ♔h6 30.♗c1
g5 31.♕e6 ♔h7 32.♖f7 ♗g7
33.♖g7, 1-0

In the next game White, following
Alekhine's suggestion, interrupted
the black pawn march at his

c3-square...then unexpectedly
launched his own Steeplechase on
the e4-e5-f6-g7 path! Black's resig-
nation was forthcoming.

Game 92
Kozlicek,L—Trangoni
Hlogovec 1994

1.e4 e5 2.♘f3 ♘c6 3.d4 ed4 4.c3
dc3 5.♘c3 ♗c5 6.♗c4 ♘f6 7.e5 d5
8.ef6 dc4 9.♕d8 ♘d8 10.fg7 ♖g8

11.♘d5!, 1-0

Two Knights Defense [C55]

A rare variant of the Max Lange attack is seen in the following game.

Game 93
Fahrni,H—Tartakower,S
Baden Baden 1914

1.e4 e5 2.♘f3 ♘c6 3.d4 ed4 4.♗c4
♘f6 5.0-0 ♗c5 6.e5 d5 7.ef6 dc4
8.fg7 ♖g8

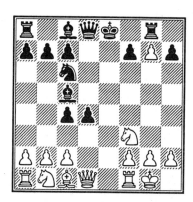

Ruy Lopez [C64]

Game 94
Akvist,H—Hvenkilde,J
Copenhagen 1974

1.e4 e5 2.♘f3 ♘c6 3.♗b5 ♗c5 4.c3
♘f6 5.d4 ♗b6 6.♗g5 ed4 7.e5 dc3
8.ef6 cb2 9.♕e2 ♕e7 10.fe7
ba1=♕

9.♗g5 ♗e7 10.♗e7 ♔e7 11.♖e1
♗e6 12.♖e4 f5 13.♖h4 ♔f7 14.♖h7
♖g7 15.♖g7 ♔g7 16.♘bd2 ♕f6
17.♕e2 c3 18.bc3 dc3 19.♘b3 ♖e8
20.♕b5 ♗c8 21.♘bd4 a6 22.♕c5
♘d4 23.♘d4 ♕e5 24.♕c3 ♔f8
25.♕d2 c5 26.♘b3 f4 27.♖f1 b5
28.♕c1 ♔f7 29.♕d1 ♗b7 30.♕d7
♖e7 31.♕h3 ♔g8 32.♕h4 c4 33.♘c1
(33.♘d2 ♗g2 34.♔g2 ♕d5 35.f3
♕d2 36.♔h1 ♖g7 37.♕h3 =;
33.♘d4 ♗g2 [33...♕d5 34.♘f3 ♖g7
35.♔h1 ♖g2 36.♖g1 ♖g1 37.♔g1
♕d1 −+] 34.♘f5 ♕f5 35.♕e7 ♗f1
36.♔f1 =, G.Marco) 33...f3 34.g3
♖d7 35.a3 ♖d4 36.♕h6 ♖d6
37.♕h4 ♗c8 38.♘a2 ♔g7 39.♘c3
♖d4 40.♘e4 ♖e4 41.♕d8 ♖e1, 0-1

11.0-0 ♘d4 12.♘d4 ♕d4 13.♘d2
c6 14.♘f3 ♕c5 15.♗d3 f6 16.♕b2
♔e7 17.♗e3 ♕h5 18.♕a3 c5
19.♖e1 ♔d8 20.♖b1 ♗c7 21.♗c5
♖e8 22.♖c1 ♖e6 23.h3 b6 24.♗e3
♗b7 25.♘d4 ♖e3 26.fe3 ♕e8
27.♗f5 g6 28.♖c7 ♔c7 29.♘b5
♔d8 30.♘d6 ♕f8 31.♘b7 ♔c7
32.♕c3 ♔b7 33.♗e4 ♔b8 34.♕c4
a5 35.♗a8 ♔a8 36.♕a6 ♔b8
37.♕b6 ♔c8 38.♕a5 ♕d6 39.♕a7,
1-0

Chigorin's Defense [D07]

An interesting theoretical byway was demonstrated by Razuvaev in this game.

Game 95
Razuvaev, Y—Koski
Mojaquec 1971

1.d4 d5 2.c4 ♘c6 3.♘f3 ♗g4 4.cd5 ♗f3 5.dc6 ♗c6 6.♘c3 e6 7.e4 ♗b4 8.f3 f5 9.♗c4 fe4? 10.0-0 ef3 11.♗e6 ♕f6 (11...fg2 [This Steeplechase ends sorrowfully] 12.♕h5 g6 13.♗f7 ♔f8 14.♗h6 ♘h6 15.♕h6 ♔e7 16.♖ae1 +–; instead, 11...♘e7 12.d5! f2 13.♖f2 ♗c5 14.♗f7 ♔f8 15.♕f3 +– was Trapl–Ratalistka, USSR 1962) **12.d5 f2** (12...♗c5 13.♔h1 fg2 [13...♖d8 14.♕f3 ♕e6 15.dc6 ±] 14.♔g2 ♕e6 15.♖e1 +–) **13.♔h1 ♗c3 14.dc6 ♕e6 15.cb7 ♖b8**

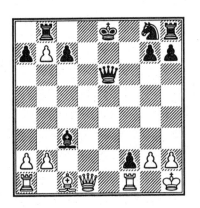

16.bc3 ♘f6 17.♕a4 ♔f7 18.♕a7 ±, 1-0

Albin's Counter Gambit [D08]

Let's confine ourselves to the examination of a well known trap. The Steeplechase d7-d5-d4-e3-f2 (and sometimes "g1" too!) puts White in a hopeless situation.

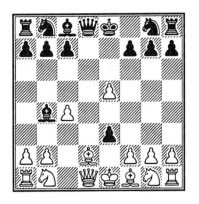

After 1.d4 d5 2.c4 e5 3.de5 d4 4.e3 ♗b4 5.♗d2 de3

Game 96
Linze—Killberg
Malmo 1917

1.d4 d5 2.c4 e5 3.de5 d4 4.e3 ♗b4 5.♗d2 de3 6.♕a4 ♘c6 7.♗b4 ef2 8.♔f2 ♕h4 9.♔e3 ♕d4 10.♔f3 ♗g4 11.♔g3 ♘h6 12.h3 ♘f5 13.♔h2 ♕f4, 0-1

Game 97
Biwer, J—Kassidi
Muncheustein 1959

1.d4 d5 2.c4 e5 3.de5 d4 4.e3 ♗b4 5.♗d2 de3 6.♗b4 ef2 7.♔e2 fg1=♘

8.♔e1 ♛h4 9.♔d2 ♘c6 10.♗c3
♗g4, 0-1

Game 98
Petrov—Pantaleev,D
Bulgaria 1973

1.d4 d5 2.c4 e5 3.de5 d4 4.e3 ♗b4
5.♗d2 de3 6.♕a4 ♘c6 7.♗b4 ef2
8.♔f2 ♛h4 9.g3 ♕d4 10.♔g2 ♕b2
11.♘d2 ♕a1 12.♘gf3 ♕b2 13.a3
♗g4, 0-1

Unfortunately, in the more serious
variation (1.d4 d5 2.c4 e5 3.de5 d4
4.♘f3 ♘c6 5.g3 ♗e6 6.♕a4 ♕d7
7.♗g2 d3 8.0-0 de2) the pawn
reaches the second rank overcoming
only one obstacle. According to our
classification, this line is not a Steeplechase, but rather an exchange
combination.

Slav Defense [D15]

Game 99
Fadeev,V—Mikheev
Furmanov 1986

1.d4 d5 2.c4 c6 3.♘c3 ♘f6 4.♘f3
dc4 5.e4 b5 6.a4 b4 7.e5 bc3 8.ef6
cb2 9.fg7 ba1=♕ 10.gh8=♕

(see next diagram)

(A mutual Excelsior has brought
about this interesting position, in

After 10.gh8=♕

which whoever has the move wins.
White to move wins with 11.♕f8
♔f8 12.♗h6 ♔e8 13.♕a1 +-)
10...♕a5 11.♘d2 ♕5c3 12.♗e2
♕ac1, 0-1

Queen's Gambit Accepted
[D21]

Game 100
Jun—Ivanchuk,V
Luzern 1993

1.d4 d5 2.c4 e6 3.♘f3 dc4 4.♕a4
♘d7 5.e4 ♘gf6 6.♘c3 a6 7.♗c4
♖b8 8.♕c2 b5 9.♗e2 ♗b7 10.0-0
b4 11.e5 bc3 12.ef6 cb2 13.fg7
ba1=♘ 14.gh8=♕ (As always, the
mutual Steeplechase leads to very
critical positions for both sides)

(see next diagram)

14...♞c2 15.♗g5 ♗f3 16.♗d8 ♗e2
17.♗c7 ♖b7 18.♗d6 ♗f1 19.♔f1
♖b6 20.♗f8 ♞f8 21.g3 ♞b4
22.♕e5 ♞d5 23.h4 ♞g6 24.♕g7 h5
25.♕g8 ♔e7 26.♕c8 ♞f8 27.a4
♞d7 28.a5 ♖d6 29.♕c4 ♔d8
30.♕e2 ♞7f6 31.♕c4 ♔d7 32.♕c5
♞e4 33.♕a3 f5 34.♔g2 ♖c6
35.♕b2 ♔c8 36.♕e2 ♞ef6 37.♕b2
f4 38.gf4 ♞f4 39.♔g3 ♞6d5
40.♕d2 ♖c3 41.f3 ♔c7 42.♕b2
♖c6 43.♕d2 ♔c8 44.♕b2 ♖c7
45.♔h2 ♖c4 46.♕a3 ♖b4 47.♕c1
♔b7 48.♕d2 ♔c6 49.♕c2 ♔b5
50.♕c5 ♔a4 51.♕c6 ♔a5 52.♕c5
♖b5 53.♕a3 ♔b6 54.♕d6 ♔a7
55.♕d7 ♖b7 56.♕d6 ♖c7 57.♔h1
a5 58.♕a3 ♔a6 59.♕b3 ♖c6
60.♔h2 ♞b6 61.♕e3 ♞fd5 62.♕e2
♞c4, 0-1

Tarrasch Defense [D32]

Game 101
Grekov,N—Grigoriev,N
Moscow 1919

1.d4 d5 2.c4 e6 3.♞c3 c5 4.♞f3
♞c6 5.♗f4 cd4 6.♞d4 ♗b4 7.♞db5
d4 8.♞c7 ♕c7 9.♗c7 dc3 10.a3 c2

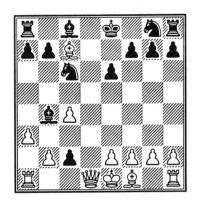

11.♕d2 ♗d2 (Black first wins back
the Queen, and then...) 12.♔d2 e5
13.♔c2 ♔d7! (Domination!), 0-1

Ragozin Defense [D39]

Game 102
Sideif-Zade—Dzhandzhava
USSR 1988

1.d4 d5 2.c4 e6 3.♞c3 ♞f6 4.♞f3
♗b4 5.♗g5 dc4 6.e4 c5 7.e5 h6
8.ef6 hg5 9.fg7 ♖g8 (We know from
the following games that in the
Ragozin defense, a Steeplechase on
the route e2-e4-e5-f6-g7 is usually
accompanied by one or two interme-

diate moves. The present game is a rare exception)

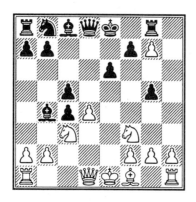

10.dc5 ♕d1 11.♖d1 ♖g7 12.♗c4 ♘c6 13.0-0 g4 14.♘d2 ♗c5 15.♘de4 ♗e7 16.♘d6 ♗d6 17.♖d6 ♔e7 18.♖fd1 ♘e5 19.♗b5 a6 20.♗e2 ♗d7 21.♖6d4 ♗c6 22.♘e4 ♖h7 23.♘g5 ♖g7 24.♘e4 ♖h8 25.♘g3 f5 26.♖e1 ♔f6 27.♗d1 ♖d7 28.♖d7 ♗d7 29.♗b3 a5 30.a4 ♘d3 31.♖d1 ♘c5 32.♘e2 ♗a4 33.♗a4 ♘a4 34.♖a1 ♘b2 35.♖a5 ♖d8 36.h3 ♖d1 37.♔h2 ♖d2 38.♘f4 gh3 39.♘h3 ♘d3 40.♔g3 b6 41.♖a3 ♘c5 42.f3 e5 43.♖a8 f4 44.♔h2 b5 45.♖f8 ♔e7 46.♖b8 ♖b2 47.♘g5 b4 48.♔h3 b3 49.g3 ♖b1 50.gf4 b2 51.♔g2 ef4 52.♖b5 ♘d3 53.♘e4 ♖c1, 0-1

Variation I

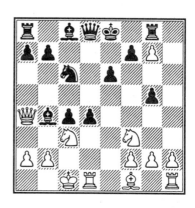

After 1.d4 ♘f6 2.c4 e6 3.♘f3 d5 4.♗g5 ♗b4 5.♘c3 dc4 6.e4 c5 7.e5 cd4 8.♕a4 ♘c6 9.0-0-0 h6 10.ef6 hg5 11.fg7 ♖g8

Game 103
Vidmar,M—Bogoljubow,E
Nottingham 1936

1.d4 ♘f6 2.c4 e6 3.♘f3 d5 4.♗g5 ♗b4 5.♘c3 dc4 6.e4 c5 7.e5 cd4 8.♕a4 ♘c6 9.0-0-0 h6 10.ef6 hg5 11.fg7 ♖g8 12.♘d4 ♗d7 13.♘e4 ♕e7 14.♘c2 f5 15.♘b4 fe4 16.♘c6 ♗c6 17.♕c4 ♖c8 18.♔b1 ♔f7 19.♗e2 ♔g7 20.♕d4 ♕f6 21.♕a7 ♖gf8 22.♕e3 ♗d5 23.♖c1 ♕f4 24.♖c8 ♖c8 25.g3 ♕e3 26.fe3 ♔f6 27.h4 gh4 28.gh4 ♔g6 29.b3 ♔h6 30.♖g1 ♖f8 31.♖g2 ♖f3 32.♗f3 ef3 33.♖f2 ♔h5 34.♔c2 ♔h4 35.♔d2 ♔g3 36.♔e1 ♗e4 37.a4 ♗c6 38.♖b2 e5 39.♖d2 ♗e8 40.♔f1 ♗c6 41.♖d6 ♗e4 42.♖f6 ♗d3 43.♔e1 ♗c2 44.a5 ♗b3 45.♖g6 ♔h4 46.♔f2 e4 47.♖d6 ♗c4

48.♖d4 ♗b5 49.♖e4 ♔h3 50.♖e7
♗c6 51.♖g7 ♔h4 52.♖g3 ♔h5
53.♖f3 ♔g5 54.♖f4 ♗h1 55.♔e1,
1-0

Game 104
Yusupov, A—Tukmakov, V
USSR 1987

1.d4 ♘f6 2.c4 e6 3.♘f3 d5 4.♘c3
dc4 5.e4 ♗b4 6.♗g5 c5 7.e5 cd4
8.♕a4 ♘c6 9.0-0-0 h6 10.ef6 hg5
11.fg7 ♖g8 12.♘d4 ♗c3 13.bc3
♕a5 14.♘c6 ♕c3 15.♔b1 bc6
16.♕c6 ♔e7 17.♕d6 ♔f6 18.♖c1
♕e5 19.♕e5 ♔e5 20.♗c4 ♗b7
21.f3 ♖g7 22.♖he1 ♔f6 23.♗b3 g4
24.♖c7 gf3 25.♖b7 fg2 26.♖g1 ♖h8
27.♗a4 ♖h2 28.♔c2 ♖g4 29.♗e8
♖h1 30.♖bb1 ♖h8 31.♗b5 ♔g5
32.♔d2 ♖b8 33.♔e3 a6 34.♗d3
♖b1 35.♗b1 ♔h4 36.♔f3 ♔h3
37.♗c2 f5, 0-1

Game 105
Timman, J—Karpov, A
Amsterdam 1987

1.d4 ♘f6 2.c4 e6 3.♘f3 d5 4.♗g5
dc4 5.♘c3 ♗b4 6.e4 c5 7.e5 cd4
8.♕a4 ♘c6 9.0-0-0 h6 10.ef6 hg5
11.fg7 ♖g8 12.♘d4 ♗c3 13.bc3
♕a5 14.♕a5 ♘a5 15.h4 g4 16.h5
♖g7 17.h6 ♖h7 18.♗e2 b6 19.♗g4
♗b7 20.♘f3 ♔e7 21.♘g5 ♖hh8
22.h7 ♗g2 23.♖h6 ♗c6 24.f4 ♗e8
25.f5 ef5 26.♗f5 ♖d8 27.♖e1 ♔f8
28.♗e4 ♔g7 29.♖h2 ♖d6 30.♖g1
♔f8 31.♖hg2 ♔e7 32.♘h3 ♗d7

33.♘f4 ♖h6 34.♖g7 ♔f6 35.♖g8
♖8h7 36.♗h7 ♖h7 37.♖e1 ♗c6
38.♖d8 ♖h4 39.♖d6 ♔g7 40.♖g1
♔f8 41.♖d4 ♖h2 42.♖d2 ♖h6
43.♖f2 ♔e7 44.♖e1 ♔d7 45.♘e2
♗d5 46.♖d1 ♖d6 47.♘d4 ♗e6
48.♖h1 a6 49.♖h8 ♗d5 50.♖d2
♔c7 51.♘f5 ♖d7 52.♘g7 ♔c6
53.♖h6 ♖d6 54.♖d6 ♔d6 55.♘e8
♔c6 56.♘f6, 1/2-1/2

Game 106
Vaisser, A—Panchenko, A
Sochi 1982

1.d4 ♘f6 2.c4 e6 3.♘f3 d5 4.♘c3
dc4 5.e4 ♗b4 6.♗g5 b5 7.a4 c6
8.e5 h6 9.ef6 hg5 10.fg7 ♖g8 11.h4
♖g7 12.hg5 ♘d7 13.♖h8 ♘f8
14.♘e5 ♗b7 15.♕f3 ♕d4 16.♘c6
♗c3 17.bc3 ♕c5 18.ab5 ♕b5
19.♕f6 ♕g5 20.♕g5 ♖g5 21.♘a5
♗g2 22.♘c4 ♗f1 23.♔f1 ♖c5
24.♘b6 ♖d8 25.♖a7 ♖c3 26.♖g8
♖cd3 27.♖b7 ♖b3 28.♔g2 ♖b2
29.♖g7 ♖d7 30.♖b8 ♖d8 31.♖b7
♖d7, 1/2-1/2

Game 107
Ribli, Z—Chernin, A
Subotica 1987

1.d4 ♘f6 2.c4 e6 3.♘f3 d5 4.♘c3
dc4 5.e4 ♗b4 6.♗g5 c5 7.e5 cd4
8.♘d4 ♕a5 9.ef6 ♗c3 10.bc3 ♕g5
11.fg7 ♕g7 12.♕f3 ♖g8 13.0-0-0
♕g4 14.♕e3 ♗d7 15.f4 ♘c6
16.♗e2 ♕g6 17.♘b5 0-0-0 18.♗f3
♕f6 19.♔b2 e5 20.♘a7 ♘a7

21.♕a7 e4 22.♗e4 ♗c6 23.♕c5
♖ge8 24.♗c6 ♕c6 25.♕c6 bc6
26.♔a3 ♖e2 27.g3 h5 28.♔b4 ♖a2
29.♔c4 ♖d1 30.♖d1 ♖h2 31.♖d6
h4 32.gh4 ♖h4 33.♖f6 ♔d8 34.♖f7
♔e8 35.♖f5 ♔e7 36.♔c5 ♔e6
37.♖e5 ♔d7 38.f5 ♖h5 39.c4 ♖g5
40.♔d4 ♖h5 41.f6 ♖h4 42.♔c5 ♖f4
43.♖e7 ♔d8 44.♖e6 ♔d7 45.♖d6
♔c7 46.♖c6 ♔d7 47.♖d6 ♔c7
48.♖e6 ♖f5 49.♔b4 ♔d7 50.♖a6
♔e8 51.♖d6 ♖f1 52.♔b5 ♖b1
53.♔c6 ♔f7 54.c5, 1-0

Game 108
Lukacs,P—Horvath,C
Hungray 1989

1.d4 ♘f6 2.c4 e6 3.♘f3 d5 4.♘c3
dc4 5.e4 ♗b4 6.♗g5 c5 7.e5 h6
8.♗d2 cd4 9.ef6 dc3 10.bc3 ♗f8
11.fg7 ♗g7 12.♗c4 ♗d7 13.0-0
♗c6 14.♖e1 ♗d5 15.♗h6 ♖h6
16.♗d5 ♘c6 17.♖b1 ♕c7 18.♕a4
0-0-0 19.♗c6 ♕c6 20.♕a7 ♖g6
21.♕e3 ♖d5 22.g3 ♖g4 23.♖b3
♕d7 24.♖b4 ♖b4 25.cb4 ♔b8
26.♖c1 e5 27.♖c5 ♖d1 28.♔g2 f6
29.♖a5 ♗f8 30.a3 ♖b1 31.♕e2
♕c6 32.♕d3, 1-0

Variation II
(The Junge System)

In this rather popular system, differ-
ent versions of the Steeplechase are
possible. Here we will examine the
two most often seen routes of march.

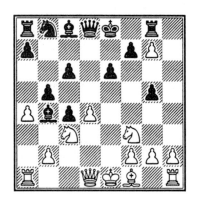

After 1.d4 d5 2.c4 e6 3.♘f3 ♘f6
4.♘c3 ♗b4 5.♗g5 dc4 6.e4 b5 7.a4
c6 8.e5 h6 9.ef6 hg5 10.fg7 ♖g8

Game 109
Popov,L—Schmidt
Varna 1968

1.d4 d5 2.c4 e6 3.♘f3 ♘f6 4.♘c3
♗b4 5.♗g5 dc4 6.e4 b5 7.a4 c6
8.e5 h6 9.ef6 hg5 10.fg7 ♖g8 11.g3
♘d7 12.♗g2 ♗b7 13.h4 gh4
14.♖h4 ♕f6 15.♔f1 ♗c3 16.bc3
♕g7 17.♘d2 ♖b8 18.ab5 cb5
19.♖a7 ♗g2 20.♔g2 ♕g5 21.♖h5
♕d8 22.♕f3 ♕b6 23.♖d7 ♔d7
24.♕f7 ♔c6 25.d5, 1-0

Game 110
Bukic,E—Pinter,J
Bajnok 1980

1.d4 d5 2.c4 e6 3.♘f3 ♘f6 4.♘c3 ♗b4 5.♗g5 dc4 6.e4 b5 7.a4 c6 8.e5 h6 9.ef6 hg5 10.fg7 ♖g8 11.g3 ♗b7 12.♗g2 ♘d7 13.h4 gh4 14.♖h4 ♖g7 15.♖h8 ♗f8 16.ab5 cb5 17.d5 ♕b6 18.♕e2 0-0-0 19.♗h3 ♗e7 20.♖d8 ♗d8 21.♘e5 ♘c5 22.♖d1 ♖h7 23.♗g2 f6 24.♘c6 ♗c6 25.dc6 b4 26.♘a4 ♘a4 27.♕e6 ♔c7 28.♕d6 ♔c8 29.♕e6 ♔c7 30.♖d8 ♕c5 31.♖d7 ♖d7 32.♕d7 ♔b6 33.c7 ♕c7 34.♕a4 ♕e5 35.♔f1 ♕b2 36.♕c6 ♔a5 37.♕c4 b3 38.♕c5 ♔a6 39.♗h3, 1-0

Game 111
Ehlvest,J—Andrianov,N
Tallin 1981

1.d4 d5 2.c4 e6 3.♘f3 ♘f6 4.♘c3 ♗b4 5.♗g5 dc4 6.e4 b5 7.a4 c6 8.e5 h6 9.ef6 hg5 10.fg7 ♖g8 11.h4 gh4 12.♖h4 ♘d7 13.♖h8 ♔e7 14.♕d2 ♖h8 15.gh8=♕ ♕h8 16.ab5 cb5 17.♘d5 ed5 18.♕b4 ♔d8 19.♕b5 ♕e8 20.♗e2 ♘b6 21.♕a5 ♔c7 22.♔f1 a6 23.♕c5 ♔b7 24.b3 ♕b5 25.♕e7 ♕d7 26.♕a3 ♕c7 27.bc4 dc4 28.♘e5 ♔a7 29.♕c5 ♕c5 30.dc5 ♘d7 31.♘d7 ♗d7 32.♗c4 ♔b7 33.♗f7 ♗b5 34.♔g1 ♔c6 35.♖c1 a5 36.♗g6 ♔c7 37.♗e4 ♗c6 38.♗c6 ♔c6 39.♔f1 a4 40.♔e2 a3 41.♔d3

a2 42.♖a1 ♔c5 43.f3 ♔b4 44.g4 ♔c5 45.♔e4 ♔d6 46.♔f5 ♔e7 47.♔g6 ♔f8 48.g5 ♖a6, 1/2-1/2

Game 112
Ehlvest,J—Tenikin
Buhara 1981

1.d4 d5 2.c4 e6 3.♘f3 ♘f6 4.♘c3 ♗b4 5.♗g5 dc4 6.e4 b5 7.a4 c6 8.e5 h6 9.ef6 hg5 10.fg7 ♖g8 11.h4 gh4 12.♖h4 ♕f6 13.♖h5 a6 14.ab5 cb5 15.♖b5 ab5 16.♖a8 ♕f4 17.♗e2 ♗b7 18.♖a7 ♗c6 19.g3 ♕e4 20.♖f7 ♘d7 21.♖f4 ♕h7 22.♘h4 ♖g7 23.♗f3 ♗d6 24.♗e4 ♕h6 25.♖f3 ♗e4 26.♘e4 ♗e7 27.♕d2 ♕h5 28.♕e2 ♕d5 29.♘c3 ♕c6 30.d5 ed5 31.♘f5 ♖f7 32.♘d4 ♕h6 33.♖f7 ♕c1 34.♘d1 ♔f7 35.♔f1 ♘f8 36.♔g2 b4 37.♕f3 ♔e8 38.♕h5 ♔d8 39.♕d5 ♔e8 40.♕h5 ♔d7 41.♕b5 ♔c7 42.♘e3, 1-0

Game 113
Tukmakov,V—Kupreichik,V
Erevan 1982

1.d4 ♘f6 2.c4 e6 3.♘f3 d5 4.♘c3 ♗b4 5.♗g5 dc4 6.e4 b5 7.a4 c6 8.e5 h6 9.ef6 hg5 10.fg7 ♖g8 11.h4 g4 12.♘e5 ♖g7 13.h5 f5 14.♗e2 ♕d5 15.♔f1 ♗c3 16.bc3 ♘d7 17.h6 ♖h7 18.♕c2 ♘e5 19.de5 ♗b7 20.♖d1 ♕e5 21.♗g4 c5 22.ab5 ♗e4 23.♗h5 ♔e7 24.♕d2 f4 25.♗f3 ♗d3 26.♔g1 ♖ah8 27.♖a1 ♕b8 28.g3 ♖g8 29.g4 e5 30.♖h5 ♖g6 31.♖e1 ♔f6 32.♖ee5

♕e5 33.♖e5 ♔e5 34.♕e1 ♔d6
35.♕e8 ♖gh6 36.♕c6 ♔e7 37.♕c5
♖d6 38.♕a7 ♔f6 39.♕b8 ♖e6
40.♕f4 ♔g6 41.♔g2 ♖e1 42.♕d6
♔g5 43.♕d8, 1-0

Game 114
Tavadian,R—Panchenko,A
Irkutsk 1983

1.d4 ♘f6 2.c4 e6 3.♘f3 d5 4.♘c3
dc4 5.e4 ♗b4 6.♗g5 b5 7.a4 c6
8.e5 h6 9.ef6 hg5 10.fg7 ♖g8 11.h4
♖g7 12.hg5 ♘d7 13.♖h8 ♘f8
14.ab5 cb5 15.♗c4 ♗c3 16.bc3 bc4
17.♕a4 ♗d7 18.♕b4 ♕e7 19.♖a7
♖d8 20.♕e7 ♔e7 21.♘e5 ♖h7
22.♘c6 ♔d6 23.♘d8, 1-0

Game 115
Lputian,S—Arbakov,V
Irkutsk 1983

1.d4 ♘f6 2.♘f3 e6 3.c4 d5 4.♘c3
dc4 5.e4 ♗b4 6.♗g5 b5 7.a4 c6
8.e5 h6 9.ef6 hg5 10.fg7 ♖g8 11.h4
gh4 12.♖h4 ♕f6 13.g3 ♘d7
14.♗g2 ♗b7 15.♔f1 a6 16.♘e5
♘e5 17.de5 ♕e5 18.ab5 ab5
19.♖a8 ♗a8 20.♕a1 ♕b8 21.♖h8,
1-0

Game 116
Yermolinsky,A—Rivas,M
Leningrad 1984

1.♘f3 d5 2.d4 ♘f6 3.c4 c6 4.♘c3
e6 5.♗g5 dc4 6.e4 b5 7.a4 ♗b4
8.e5 h6 9.ef6 hg5 10.fg7 ♖g8 11.h4

gh4 12.♖h4 ♕f6 13.g3 ♘d7
14.♗g2 ♗b7 15.♔f1 ♘c3 16.bc3 a6
17.♘e5 ♘e5 18.de5 ♕e5 19.ab5
ab5 20.♖a8 ♗a8 21.♕a1 ♕b8
22.♖h8 ♔d7 23.♖g8 ♕g8 24.♕a7
♔d6 25.♕a3 b4 26.♕b4 c5 27.♕b6
♔e5 28.♕c5 ♔f6 29.♕d4 e5
30.♕h4, 1-0

Game 117
Wirthensohn,H—Flear,G
Graz 1984

1.c4 e6 2.d4 d5 3.♘f3 ♘f6 4.♗g5
c6 5.♘c3 dc4 6.e4 b5 7.a4 ♗b4
8.e5 h6 9.ef6 hg5 10.fg7 ♖g8 11.h4
gh4 12.♖h4 ♕f6 13.g3 ♘d7
14.♗g2 ♗b7 15.♔f1 ♗c3 16.bc3
♕g7 17.♘e5 ♘e5 18.de5 ♕e5
19.ab5 ♖d8 20.♖d4 ♖d4 21.♕d4
♕b5 22.♕a7 ♔e7 23.♕a3 ♔f6
24.♕c1 c5 25.♕f4 ♔g6 26.♕g4
♔h7 27.♕h5 ♔g7 28.♕e5 ♔g6
29.♗e4 ♗e4 30.♕e4 ♔f6 31.♕f4
♔g6 32.♕g4 ♔h7 33.♕h5 ♔g7
34.♕e5 ♔g6 35.♕e4 ♔f6 36.♖b1
♕d7 37.♕f3 ♔g6 38.♕g4 ♔f6
39.♕f3 ♔g6 40.♖d1 ♕c7 41.♕g4,
1-0

Game 118
Salov,V—Neverov,V
Volvograd 1985

1.d4 d5 2.c4 e6 3.♘f3 ♘f6 4.♘c3
♗b4 5.♗g5 dc4 6.e4 b5 7.a4 c6
8.e5 h6 9.ef6 hg5 10.fg7 ♖g8 11.h4
g4 12.♘e5 f5 13.f3 c5 14.dc5 ♕f6
15.♕e2 ♖g7 16.ab5 ♘d7 17.f4 ♘e5

18.♕e5 ♕e5 19.fe5 ♗c5 20.♗c4
♗b7 21.♔f1 ♖d8 22.h5 ♖d2
23.♘e2, 1-0

Game 119
Averkin,O—Bagirov,V
Volvograd 1985

1.d4 d5 2.c4 e6 3.♘f3 ♘f6 4.♘c3
♗b4 5.♗g5 dc4 6.e4 b5 7.a4 c6
8.e5 h6 9.ef6 hg5 10.fg7 ♖g8
11.h4 ♘d7 12.hg5 ♗b7 13.♖h8
♔e7 14.♖h7 ♕a5 15.♗e2 ♗c3
16.bc3 ♕c3 17.♔f1 a6 18.♖c1 ♕a3
19.♕d2 c5 20.♘e5 cd4 21.♘d7
♔d7 22.♕d4 ♗d5 23.♖a1 ♕d6
24.♖d1, 1-0

Game 120
Loginov,V—Panchenko,A
Aktjubinsk 1985

1.♘f3 ♘f6 2.c4 e6 3.♘c3 d5 4.d4
dc4 5.e4 ♗b4 6.♗g5 b5 7.a4 c6
8.e5 h6 9.ef6 hg5 10.fg7 ♖g8
11.h4 ♘d7 12.hg5 ♗b7 13.ab5 cb5
14.♖h8 ♔e7 15.♕d2 a5 16.d5 ♖h8
17.d6 ♗d6 18.0-0-0 ♖a6 19.gh8=♕
♕h8 20.♘b5 ♕b8 21.♘d6 ♖d6
22.♕d6 ♕d6 23.♖d6 ♔d6 24.♗c4
♗f3 25.gf3 ♔c5 26.♗e2 ♔d4
27.♔c2 ♘c5 28.♗b5 e5, 0-1

Game 121
Ragozin,V—Baburin,A
Tomsk 1986

1.d4 d5 2.c4 e6 3.♘f3 ♘f6 4.♘c3
♗b4 5.♗g5 dc4 6.e4 b5 7.a4 c6

8.e5 h6 9.ef6 hg5 10.fg7 ♖g8 11.h4
gh4 12.♖h4 ♕f6 13.♕c2 ♗b7
14.♕e4 ♕g6 15.♕g6 fg6 16.♖h8
♔f7 17.♘g5 ♔g7 18.♖h7 ♔f6
19.♘ge4, 1-0

Game 122
Zakharevich,I—Sabyanov
Andropov 1986

1.d4 d5 2.c4 e6 3.♘f3 ♘f6 4.♘c3
♗b4 5.♗g5 dc4 6.e4 b5 7.a4 c6
8.e5 h6 9.ef6 hg5 10.fg7 ♖g8
11.h4 g4 12.♘e5 f5 13.g3 ♗b7
14.♗g2 ♕c7 15.0-0 ♗c3 16.bc3
♖g7 17.♖e1 ♘d7 18.♘c6 ♕d6
19.d5 e5 20.♕d4 ♖e7 21.♘e7 ♔e7
22.ab5 ♔f7 23.♕c4, 1-0

Game 123
Lermahn—Karpov,Al
USSR 1986

1.d4 d5 2.c4 e6 3.♘f3 ♘f6 4.♘c3
♗b4 5.♗g5 dc4 6.e4 b5 7.a4 c6
8.e5 h6 9.ef6 hg5 10.fg7 ♖g8
11.h4 g4 12.♘e5 ♖g7 13.h5 f5
14.♗e2 ♕d5 15.♕d2 ♘d7 16.h6
♖h7 17.♕g5 ♘f8 18.f3 c5 19.0-0-0
♗c3 20.bc3 ♗d7 21.fg4 f4 22.♗f3
♕d6 23.d5 ♖b8 24.de6 ♕e6
25.♖he1 ♖e7 26.♘d7, 1-0

Game 124
Hauzman,A—Oll,L
Uzhgorod 1987

1.♘f3 ♘f6 2.c4 e6 3.♘c3 d5 4.d4
dc4 5.e4 ♗b4 6.♗g5 b5 7.a4 c6

8.e5 h6 9.ef6 hg5 10.fg7 ♖g8
11.g3 ♗b7 12.♗g2 ♘d7 13.0-0 a6
14.ab5 ab5 15.♖a8 ♗a8 16.♘e5
♘e5 17.de5 ♖g7 18.♘e4 ♕d1
19.♖d1 f5 20.ef6 ♖a7 21.♘g5 c5
22.f7 ♔e7 23.♖d8, 1-0

Game 125
Kanstler,B—Oll,L
Uzhgorod 1987

1.d4 ♘f6 2.♘f3 d5 3.c4 e6 4.♘c3
dc4 5.e4 ♗b4 6.♗g5 b5 7.a4 c6
8.e5 h6 9.ef6 hg5 10.fg7 ♖g8
11.g3 ♗b7 12.♗g2 c5 13.dc5 ♕d1
14.♔d1 g4 15.♘e1 ♗g2 16.♘g2
ba4 17.♖a4 ♘c6 18.♘e3 ♖g7
19.♘c4 ♗c5 20.♘e4 ♗d4 21.♖a6
♘b4 22.♖a4 ♘c6 23.♖a6 ♘b4
24.♖a4, 0-1

Game 126
Dokhoian,Y—Yakovich,Y
Uzhgorod 1987

1.d4 d5 2.♘f3 ♘f6 3.c4 dc4 4.♘c3
e6 5.e4 ♗b4 6.♗g5 b5 7.a4 c6
8.e5 h6 9.ef6 hg5 10.fg7 ♖g8
11.h4 g4 12.♘e5 ♖g7 13.h5 f5
14.♗e2 c5 15.h6 ♖h7 16.♗g4 ♕d4
17.♗h5 ♔e7 18.♘g6 ♔f6 19.♕c1
♗c3 20.bc3 ♕e4 21.♔f1 ♗b7
22.♗f3 ♕d3 23.♗e2 ♕d6 24.♖h3
♔g6 25.♖g3 ♕g3 26.fg3 ♖h6
27.♕b2 ♖h2 28.♖d1 ♘a6 29.♕b5
♗g2 30.♔e1 ♘c7 31.♕c4 ♘d5
32.g4 f4 33.♕c5 ♖f8 34.♕f8, 1-0

Game 127
Lobron,E—Werner,M
Cannes 1988

1.d4 ♘f6 2.♘f3 e6 3.c4 d5 4.♘c3
dc4 5.e4 ♗b4 6.♗g5 b5 7.a4 c6
8.e5 h6 9.ef6 hg5 10.fg7 ♖g8
11.g3 ♗b7 12.♗g2 ♘d7 13.0-0 a6
14.ab5 cb5 15.♘g5 ♗g2 16.♕h5
♕e7 17.♔g2 ♗c3 18.bc3 ♘f6
19.♕f3 ♘d5 20.♘e4 ♖g7 21.♖fb1
♕d8 22.♖a2 ♔e7 23.h4 ♕c8
24.♔g1 ♕c6 25.♘f6 ♖g6 26.♘d5
ed5 27.♖e1 ♖e6 28.♖e6 fe6 29.h5
♕e8 30.♖e2 ♔d7 31.♖e5 ♕g8
32.h6 ♖e8 33.♕f6 ♕h8 34.♖e6
♕f6 35.♖f6 b4 36.cb4 c3 37.♖a6
♖e1 38.♔g2 c2 39.♖a7 ♔d6
40.♖a6 ♔d7 41.h7 ♖g1 42.♔g1
c1=♕ 43.♔g2, 1-0

Game 128
Moreno—Mendez
Havana 1996

1.d4 d5 2.c4 e6 3.♘f3 ♘f6 4.♘c3
♗b4 5.♗g5 dc4 6.e4 b5 7.a4 c6
8.e5 h6 9.ef6 hg5 10.fg7 ♖g8 11.h4
gh4 12.♖h4 ♕f6 13.♕c2 ♗b7
14.♕e4 a6 15.ab5 ab5 16.♖a8 ♗a8
17.♕e5 ♕e5 18.♘e5 ♖g7 19.♖h8
♗f8 20.♘e4 c5 21.♘f6 ♔e7
22.♘h5 ♖g5 23.f4 ♖h5 24.♖h5 cd4
25.♖h7 ♔e8 26.♖f7 ♗e4 27.♗e2
♘c6 28.♗h5 ♘e5 29.fe5 ♗b4
30.♔d1 ♔d8 31.♗f3 ♗g6 32.♖f6
♗b1 33.♖e6, 0-1

Game 129
Gabriel,C—Kupreichik,V
Bad Woerishofen 1997

1.d4 ♘f6 2.c4 e6 3.♘f3 d5 4.♘c3
dc4 5.e4 ♗b4 6.♗g5 b5 7.a4 c6
8.e5 h6 9.ef6 hg5 10.fg7 ♖g8
11.g3 ♗b7 12.♗g2 ♘d7 13.0-0 a6
14.♘e5 ♕c7 15.ab5 cb5 16.♗b7
♕b7 17.♘d7 ♕d7 18.♕f3 ♔e7
19.d5 ♗c3 20.de6 fe6 21.♕c3 ♕d3
22.♕e5 ♕f5 23.♕d4 ♔f7 24.♕d7
♔f6 25.♖fe1 ♖ad8 26.♕c7 ♖d2
27.♕b6 ♖g7 28.♖a6 ♖e7 29.♕e3
♕d5 30.h4 gh4 31.♕h6 ♔f7
32.♕h7 ♔f6 33.♕h4 ♔f7 34.♕h7
♔f6 35.♕h8 ♔g6 36.♖a8 ♖g7
37.♖a6 ♖e2 38.♕e8 ♔f6 39.♕f8
♔g6 40.♖e2 ♕d1 41.♔g2 ♕e2
42.♕e8, 0-1

Variation III

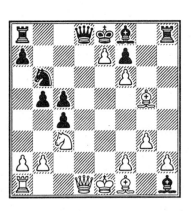

After 1.d4 d5 2.c4 e6 3.♘c3 ♘f6
4.♘f3 c6 5.♗g5 dc4 6.e4 b5 7.e5 h6
8.♗h4 g5 9.♘g5 hg5 10.♗g5 ♘bd7

11.ef6 ♗b7 12.g3 c5 13.d5 ♘b6
14.de6 ♗h1 15.e7

Game 130
Smejkal,J—Bednarsky,J
Sweden 1975

1.d4 d5 2.c4 e6 3.♘c3 ♘f6 4.♘f3
c6 5.♗g5 dc4 6.e4 b5 7.e5 h6
8.♗h4 g5 9.♘g5 hg5 10.♗g5 ♘bd7
11.ef6 ♗b7 12.g3 c5 13.d5 ♘b6
14.de6 ♗h1 15.e7 ♕d1 16.♖d1 a6
17.ef8=♕ ♖f8 18.♖d6 ♘d7 19.♗f4
0-0-0 20.♗h3 ♖h8 21.♗g4 ♖h2
22.♖b6 ♖e8 23.♔f1 ♗b7 24.♗d7
♔d7 25.♖b7 ♔e6 26.g4 ♖h4
27.♖b6 ♔d7 28.f3 b4 29.♘e4 ♖c8
30.♖a6 ♖c6 31.♖a7 ♔e6 32.♖a5
♔d5 33.♗e3 c3 34.bc3 ♔c4 35.cb4
cb4 36.♘d2 ♔c3 37.♘e4 ♔d3
38.♗f2 ♖h1 39.♔g2 ♖a1 40.♘c5
♔c4 41.♘b3 ♖d1 42.g5 ♖d5
43.♖d5, 1-0

Game 131
Bareev,E—Lukacs,P
Vrnjacka Banja 1987

1.d4 ♘f6 2.c4 e6 3.♘f3 d5 4.♘c3
c6 5.♗g5 dc4 6.e4 b5 7.e5 h6
8.♗h4 g5 9.♘g5 hg5 10.♗g5 ♘bd7
11.ef6 ♗b7 12.g3 c5 13.d5 ♘b6
14.de6 ♗h1 15.e7 ♕d7 16.f3 ♗e7
17.fe7 f6 18.♗f6 ♖h2 19.♘e4 ♘d5
20.a4 ♕e6 21.♗h4 ♘e7 22.♗e2
♖d8 23.♕c1 ♖d3 24.♕g5 ♗f3
25.♗f3 ♖f3 26.♕h5 ♖f7 27.♕h8
♖f8 28.♕h5 ♕g6 29.♕e5 ♖h4, 0-1

Variation IV

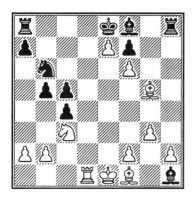

After 1.d4 d5 2.c4 e6 3.♘c3 ♘f6 4.♘f3 c6 5.♗g5 dc4 6.e4 b5 7.e5 h6 8.♗h4 g5 9.♘g5 hg5 10.♗g5 ♘bd7 11.ef6 ♗b7 12.g3 c5 13.d5 ♘b6 14.de6 ♕d1 15.♖d1 ♗h1 16.e7

Game 132
Plachetka,J—Bagirov,V
Berlin 1979

1.d4 d5 2.c4 e6 3.♘c3 ♘f6 4.♘f3 c6 5.♗g5 dc4 6.e4 b5 7.e5 h6 8.♗h4 g5 9.♘g5 hg5 10.♗g5 ♘bd7 11.ef6 ♗b7 12.g3 c5 13.d5 ♘b6 14.de6 ♕d1 15.♖d1 ♗h1 16.e7 a6 17.ef8=♕ ♔f8 18.♗e3 ♖h5 19.♖d6 ♖b8 20.♗e2 ♖e5 21.♔d2 b4 22.♘d1 ♔g8 23.♗f4 ♖ee8 24.♘e3 c3 25.bc3 bc3 26.♔c3 ♘a4 27.♔d2 ♖b2 28.♔e1 ♘c3 29.♗d3 ♖a2 30.♖a6 ♖a6 31.♗a6 ♘d5 32.♗b5 ♖e6 33.♗c4 ♘f4 34.gf4 ♖f6 35.f5 ♗e4 36.♘g4 ♖d6 37.f6 ♗f3 38.♘e3 ♖f6, 0-1

Game 133
Beliavsky,A—Bagirov,V
Moscow 1981

1.d4 ♘f6 2.c4 e6 3.♘f3 d5 4.♘c3 c6 5.♗g5 dc4 6.e4 b5 7.e5 h6 8.♗h4 g5 9.♘g5 hg5 10.♗g5 ♘bd7 11.ef6 ♗b7 12.g3 c5 13.d5 ♘b6 14.de6 ♕d1 15.♖d1 ♗h1 16.e7 a6 17.ef8=♕ ♔f8 18.♖d6 ♖b8 19.♗e3 ♖h5 20.♗e2 ♖e5 21.♘d1 ♔g8 22.♗f4 ♖ee8 23.♘e3 ♗e4 24.f3 ♗g6 25.h4 ♖b7 26.g4 ♘a4 27.h5 ♗b1 28.b3 ♘c3 29.bc4 ♗a2 30.♗d3 ♗c4 31.♗c4 bc4 32.g5 ♔h7 33.g6 ♔g8 34.♔f1 ♘b5 35.♖a6 ♘d4 36.♘g4 ♘f5 37.♘e5 c3 38.♖c6 ♖f8 39.♗g5 ♘g3 40.♔g2 ♘h5 41.g7 ♖fb8 42.♘g4 ♔h7 43.♘h6 ♔g6 44.♖c5 ♘f6 45.♗f6 ♔h6 46.♗e5 ♖g8 47.♖c6 ♔h7 48.♗c3 ♖bb8 49.♗e5 ♖bc8 50.♖b6 ♖g7, 0-1

Game 134
Polugaevsky,L—Torre,E
Moscow 1981

1.d4 d5 2.c4 c6 3.♘f3 ♘f6 4.♘c3 e6 5.♗g5 dc4 6.e4 b5 7.e5 h6 8.♗h4 g5 9.♘g5 hg5 10.♗g5 ♘bd7 11.ef6 ♗b7 12.g3 c5 13.d5 ♘b6 14.de6 ♕d1 15.♖d1 ♗h1 16.e7 a6 17.h4 ♗h6 18.f4 b4 19.♖d6 ♖b8 20.♘d1 ♗g5 21.fg5 ♘d5 22.♗c4 ♘e7 23.fe7 ♔e7 24.♖f6 ♖hf8 25.♘e3 ♗e4 26.♖a6 ♖bd8 27.♖f6 ♖d6 28.♖f4 ♖d4 29.h5 ♗d3 30.♘d5 ♔d6 31.♖d4 cd4 32.♗b3

♗c2 33.♗c2 ♔d5 34.♗b3 ♔e5 35.g4 ♔f4 36.g6 ♔e3 37.g7 ♖c8 38.♔f1 d3 39.♔g2 ♔f4 40.h6 (Time), 1-0

Game 135
Suba,M—Tatai,S
Dortmund 1981

1.c4 ♘f6 2.♘c3 e6 3.♘f3 d5 4.d4 c6 5.♗g5 dc4 6.e4 b5 7.e5 h6 8.♗h4 g5 9.♘g5 hg5 10.♗g5 ♘bd7 11.g3 ♕b6 12.ef6 c5 13.♗g2 ♗b7 14.d5 b4 15.0-0 0-0-0 16.de6 ♗g2 17.e7

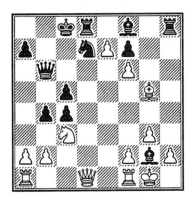

17...♗f1 18.♘d5 ♕b7 19.ed8=♕ ♔d8 20.♔f1 ♖h2 21.♔g1 ♖h8 22.♕f3 ♗d6 23.♖d1 ♗e5 24.♕e2 c3 25.bc3 bc3 26.♕e4 ♖e8 27.♕h1, 0-1

Variation V

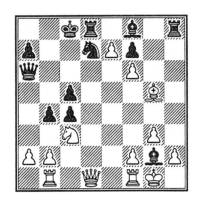

After 1.c4 c6 2.d4 d5 3.♘c3 ♘f6 4.♘f3 e6 5.♗g5 dc4 6.e4 b5 7.e5 h6 8.♗h4 g5 9.♘g5 hg5 10.♗g5 ♘bd7 11.g3 ♗b7 12.♗g2 ♕b6 13.ef6 0-0-0 14.0-0 c5 15.d5 b4 16.♖b1 ♕a6 17.de6 ♗g2 18.e7

Game 136
Uhlmann,W—Alexandria,N
Halle 1981

1.c4 c6 2.d4 d5 3.♘c3 ♘f6 4.♘f3 e6 5.♗g5 dc4 6.e4 b5 7.e5 h6 8.♗h4 g5 9.♘g5 hg5 10.♗g5 ♘bd7 11.g3 ♗b7 12.♗g2 ♕b6 13.ef6 0-0-0 14.0-0 c5 15.d5 b4 16.♖b1 ♕a6 17.de6 ♗g2 18.e7 ♗f1 19.♔f1 bc3 20.♕d5 ♗e7 21.fe7 c2 22.ed8=♕ ♖d8 23.♖c1 c3 24.♔g2 cb2 25.♕a8 ♘b8 26.♖c2 ♕b6 27.♗d8 ♔d8 28.♕d5 ♘d7 29.♖d2 ♕b5 30.a4, 1-0

Game 137
Yermolinsky, A—Shabalov, A
USSR 1986

1.d4 d5 2.c4 e6 3.♘c3 ♘f6 4.♘f3 c6 5.♗g5 dc4 6.e4 b5 7.e5 h6 8.♗h4 g5 9.♘g5 hg5 10.♗g5 ♘bd7 11.ef6 ♗b7 12.g3 c5 13.d5 ♛b6 14.♗g2 b4 15.0-0 0-0-0 16.♖b1 ♛a6 17.de6 ♗g2 18.e7 ♗a8 19.ed8=♛ ♚d8 20.♘e2 ♚c8 21.♛c2 ♛e6 22.♘f4 ♛g4 23.♖fe1 ♗h6 24.♗h6 ♛f3 25.♚f1 ♛h1 26.♚e2 ♛f3 27.♚d2 ♛f2 28.♖e2 ♛d4 29.♚c1 ♗f3 30.♗g7 ♖h2 31.♖h2 ♛g1 32.♚d2 ♛h2, 0-1

Game 138
Yermolinsky, A—Ivanchuk, V
Pinsk 1986

1.d4 d5 2.c4 e6 3.♘c3 ♘f6 4.♘f3 c6 5.♗g5 dc4 6.e4 b5 7.e5 h6 8.♗h4 g5 9.♘g5 hg5 10.♗g5 ♘bd7 11.ef6 ♗b7 12.g3 c5 13.d5 ♛b6 14.♗g2 b4 15.0-0 0-0-0 16.♖b1 ♛a6 17.de6 ♗g2 18.e7 ♗f1 19.♛d5 ♗h6 20.ed8=♛ ♚d8 21.♘e4 ♗h3 22.♘c5 ♗e6 23.♘e6 fe6 24.♛a8 ♛c8 25.♛a7 ♗g5 26.♛a5 ♛c7 27.♛g5 ♛e5 28.♛d2 c3 29.bc3 bc3 30.♛d3 ♛f5 31.♛f5 ef5 32.♖c1 ♘f6 33.♖c3 ♚e7 34.a4 ♖a8 35.♖a3 ♖a5 36.♚g2 f4 37.h4 ♚e6 38.♚f3 ♚f5 39.♖a1 ♘g4 40.gf4, 0-1

Game 139
Yermolinsky, A—Gurevich, D
USA 1994

1.♘f3 d5 2.d4 ♘f6 3.c4 c6 4.♘c3 e6 5.♗g5 dc4 6.e4 b5 7.e5 h6 8.♗h4 g5 9.♘g5 hg5 10.♗g5 ♘bd7 11.g3 ♗b7 12.♗g2 ♛b6 13.ef6 c5 14.d5 0-0-0 15.0-0 b4 16.♖b1 ♛a6 17.de6 ♗g2 18.e7 ♗f1 19.♛d5 ♗h6 20.♗h6 ♗d3 21.♛a8 ♘b8 22.ed8=♛ ♖d8 23.♖e1 bc3 24.♗f4 ♛b6 25.bc3 ♗f5 26.h4 ♗e6 27.♚h2 ♖d7 28.h5 ♖b7 29.♗b8 ♖b8 30.♛e4 ♚c7 31.♖d1 ♖h8 32.g4 ♛b2 33.♛f4 ♚b7 34.♛f3 ♚c7 35.♛f4 ♚c6 36.♛e4 ♚c7 37.♛e5 ♚b6 38.♖d6 ♚b7 39.♛e4 ♚b8 40.♛f4 ♚b7 41.♛f3 ♚c7 42.♛f4 ♚b7 43.♛f3 ♚c7 44.♖c6 ♚d7 45.♖c5 ♛b6 46.♖e5 ♛d6 47.♛b7 ♚d8 48.♛a8 ♗c8 49.♛d5 ♛d5 50.♖d5 ♚e8 51.♚g3 ♖h6 52.♖d6 ♗e6 53.f4 ♖h8 54.♚h4 ♗d7 55.f5 ♚d8 56.♖a6 ♖e8 57.♖a7 ♖e4 58.♖a8 ♚c7 59.♚g5 ♖e3 60.h6 ♗c8 61.♖a4 ♚d6 62.♖c4 ♗d7 63.a4, 1-0

Game 140
Beliavsky, A—Shirov, A
Ljubljana 1995

1.d4 d5 2.c4 c6 3.♘c3 ♘f6 4.♘f3 e6 5.♗g5 dc4 6.e4 b5 7.e5 h6 8.♗h4 g5 9.♘g5 hg5 10.♗g5 ♘bd7 11.ef6 ♗b7 12.g3 c5 13.d5 ♛b6 14.♗g2 b4 15.0-0 0-0-0 16.♖b1 ♛a6 17.de6 ♗g2 18.e7 ♗f1

19.♕d5 ♗h6 20.♗h6 ♗d3 21.♘e4
♗e4 22.♕e4 ♖de8 23.♗g7 ♖h5
24.♖d1 ♕b5 25.f4 c3 26.bc3 c4
27.cb4 ♔c7 28.g4 ♖h3 29.g5 ♖d3
30.♖c1 c3 31.g6 fg6 32.f7 ♖e7
33.♕e7 ♕b6 34.♔f1 ♕b5 35.♕e2
♕c4 36.♔e1 ♔b7 37.♕g2 ♔c7
38.♕e2 ♔b7 39.♕g2 ♔c7 40.♕e2 ,
0-1

Game 141
Kamsky,G—Kramnik,V
Dos Hermanas 1996

1.d4 d5 2.c4 c6 3.♘c3 ♘f6 4.♘f3
e6 5.♗g5 dc4 6.e4 b5 7.e5 h6
8.♗h4 g5 9.♘g5 hg5 10.♗g5 ♘bd7
11.ef6 ♗b7 12.g3 c5 13.d5 ♕b6
14.♗g2 0-0-0 15.0-0 b4 16.♖b1
♕a6 17.de6 ♗g2 18.e7 ♗f1 19.♔f1
♗e7 20.fe7 ♖dg8 21.♘e4 ♕c6
22.♘d6 ♔b8 23.♗f4 ♖h2 24.♔e2
♔a8 25.♕c2 ♘b6 26.♕f5 ♘c8
27.e8=♕ ♖e8 28.♘e8 ♕e8 29.♗e3
♘b6 30.♖d1 ♔b7 31.♕c5 ♕a4
32.♖d2 c3 33.bc3 bc3 34.♖d4 ♕a2
35.♔f3 c2 36.♖d2 ♖h8 37.♖c2 ♕d5
38.♕d5 ♘d5 39.♖b2 ♘b6 40.♔e4
♖c8 41.g4 ♖c6 42.g5 ♖e6 43.♔f5
a5 44.♖b5 a4 45.♖a5 ♘c4 46.♖a4
♘e3 47.fe3 ♖e3 48.♖a5 ♔c6
49.♔f6 ♖f3 50.♔e7 ♖f1 51.♖a6
♔d5 52.♖f6 ♖g1 53.♖f5 ♔e4
54.♔f6 ♖g4 55.♖e5 ♔d4, 0-1

Game 142
Grunberg—Shuganev
Timishoara 1996

1.d4 d5 2.c4 e6 3.♘c3 ♘f6 4.♘f3
c6 5.♗g5 dc4 6.e4 b5 7.e5 h6
8.♗h4 g5 9.♘g5 hg5 10.♗g5 ♘bd7
11.ef6 ♗b7 12.g3 c5 13.d5 ♕b6
14.♗g2 b4 15.0-0 0-0-0 16.♖b1
♕a6 17.de6 ♗g2 18.e7 ♗f1
19.♕d5 ♗h6 20.♗h6 ♗d3 21.♘e4
♗e4 22.♕e4 ♖de8 23.♗g7 ♖h5
24.♖d1 ♕a4 25.b3 cb3 26.ab3 ♕b5
27.f4 c4 28.bc4 ♕b6 29.♔g2 ♖a5
30.g4 b3 31.g5 ♖a2 32.♔h1 b2
33.♕d5 ♕b7, 0-1

Game 143
Nikolic,P—Shirov,A
Linares 1997

1.d4 d5 2.c4 c6 3.♘c3 ♘f6 4.♘f3
e6 5.♗g5 dc4 6.e4 b5 7.e5 h6
8.♗h4 g5 9.♘g5 hg5 10.♗g5 ♘bd7
11.ef6 ♗b7 12.g3 c5 13.d5 ♕b6
14.♗g2 b4 15.0-0 0-0-0 16.♖b1
♕a6 17.de6 ♗g2 18.e7 ♗f1 19.♔f1
♕c6 20.ed8=♕ ♔d8 21.♘d5 ♖h2
22.♔g1 ♖h8 23.♗f4 ♕e6 24.♕f3
♕h3 25.♖d1 b3 26.a4 ♕h2 27.♔f1
♕h1 28.♔e2 ♕f3 29.♔f3 ♔c8
30.g4 ♖h3 31.♔e4 c3 32.bc3 c4
33.♘e7 ♔d8 34.♘c6 ♔e8 35.♗g3
♘c5 36.♔d5 ♘d3 37.♖b1 ♔d7
38.♘b8 ♔c8 39.♔c4 ♘c5 40.♘c6
♘e4 41.♘e7 ♔d7 42.♖d1 ♔e8
43.♘d5 ♗d6 44.♖e1, 1-0

Game 144
Ubilava,E—Timoshenko,Gen
Volgodonsk 1981

1.d4 d5 2.c4 c6 3.♘f3 ♘f6 4.♘c3
e6 5.♗g5 dc4 6.e4 b5 7.e5 h6
8.♗h4 g5 9.♘g5 hg5 10.♗g5 ♘bd7
11.ef6 ♗b7 12.g3 c5 13.d5 ♕b6
14.♗g2 0-0-0 15.0-0 b4 16.♘a4
♕b5 17.de6 ♗g2 18.e7

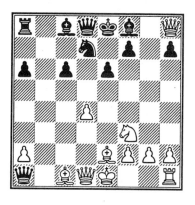

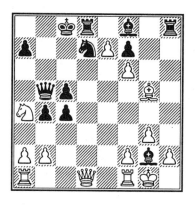

18...♗f1 19.ed8=♕ ♔d8 20.♔f1
♕c6 21.♔g1 ♗d6 22.f4 ♖e8 23.♔f2
♔c7 24.b3 cb3 25.ab3 c4 26.♕d4
♘b6 27.g4 ♖e4 28.♕d1 ♘a4
29.♖a4 ♗c5 30.♔g3 ♖e3 31.♔h4
♕g2, 0-1

Semi-Slav Defense [D47]

Here the mutual Excelsior along the
main diagonal leads, as a rule, to positions favorable to White.

(see next diagram)

After 1.d4 d5 2.c4 e6 3.♘c3 c6
4.♘f3 ♘f6 5.e3 ♘bd7 6.♗d3 dc4
7.♗c4 b5 8.♗e2 a6 9.e4 b4 10.e5
bc3 11.ef6 cb2 12.fg7 ba1=♕
13.gh8=♕

Game 145
Krogius,N—Kamyshov,M
Taroslare 1949

1.d4 d5 2.c4 e6 3.♘c3 c6 4.♘f3
♘f6 5.e3 ♘bd7 6.♗d3 dc4 7.♗c4
b5 8.♗e2 a6 9.e4 b4 10.e5 bc3
11.ef6 cb2 12.fg7 ba1=♕ 13.gh8=♕
♕a5 14.♘d2 ♕f5 15.0-0 ♗b7
16.♕b3 ♘c5 17.♗a3 ♘b3 18.♕f8
♔d7 19.♕e7 ♔c8 20.♘b3 ♕f1
21.♗f1 ♕d5 22.♗d6, 1-0

Game 146
Benko,P—Pytel,K
Hastings 1973

1.♘f3 d5 2.c4 c6 3.e3 ♘f6 4.♘c3
e6 5.d4 ♘bd7 6.♗d3 dc4 7.♗c4 b5
8.♗e2 a6 9.e4 b4 10.e5 bc3 11.ef6
cb2 12.fg7 ba1=♕ 13.gh8=♕ ♕a5

14.♗d2 ♕d1 15.♗d1 ♕f5 16.0-0
♗b7 17.d5 ♕d5 18.♕h7 c5 19.♗a4
0-0-0 20.♗a5 ♘e5 21.♘e1 c4
22.♗d8 ♕d8 23.♕h8 f6 24.♕g8
♕d6 25.♘c2 ♔c7 26.♘e3 ♗e7
27.♖d1 ♕b6 28.♕e8 ♗c5
29.♕d8#, 1-0

The Modern Line

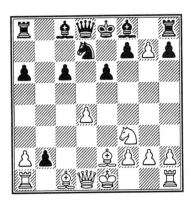

After 1.d4 d5 2.c4 e6 3.♘c3 c6
4.♘f3 ♘f6 5.e3 ♘bd7 6.♗d3 dc4
7.♗c4 b5 8.♗e2 a6 9.e4 b4 10.e5
bc3 11.ef6 cb2 12.fg7

Game 147
Taimanov,M—Onat,I
Albena 1974

1.d4 d5 2.c4 e6 3.♘c3 c6 4.♘f3
♘f6 5.e3 ♘bd7 6.♗d3 dc4 7.♗c4
b5 8.♗e2 a6 9.e4 b4 10.e5 bc3
11.ef6 cb2 12.fg7 ♗g7 13.♗b2 c5
14.0-0 ♗b7 15.♖b1 ♗e4 16.dc5
♗b1 17.♗g7 ♖g8 18.c6 ♘c5
19.♗d4 ♗a2 20.♗c5 ♗d5 21.♕a4

♕c7 22.♕h4 ♗c6 23.♕h7 0-0-0
24.♗a6 ♔b8 25.♗e2, 1-0

Game 148
Bukhman,E—Karasev,V
Kronstadt 1975

1.d4 d5 2.c4 e6 3.♘c3 c6 4.♘f3 ♘f6
5.e3 ♘bd7 6.♗d3 dc4 7.♗c4 b5
8.♗e2 a6 9.e4 b4 10.e5 bc3 11.ef6
cb2 12.fg7 ♗g7 13.♗b2 ♕a5
14.♘d2 ♕b4 15.♕c2 ♗d4 16.♗d4
♕d4 17.0-0 ♖b8 18.♘b3 ♕g7
19.♖ad1 c5 20.♖d3 ♗b7 21.♖g3
♕e5 22.f4 ♗e4 23.♕d2 ♕c7
24.♕c3 ♔e7 25.♕e3 ♗d5 26.♖g5
♗b3 27.ab3 h6 28.♖g3 c4 29.♗c4
♕c5 30.♖a1 ♕e3 31.♖e3 ♘c5
32.f5 ♖b6 33.fe6 fe6 34.♔f2 ♖f8
35.♔e2 ♖fb8 36.♖a3 ♖g8 37.g3
♖f8 38.♖a5 ♔d6 39.♔d2 ♖f2
40.♔c3 e5 41.b4 ♘d7 42.♖d3 ♔c7
43.♖ad5 ♖f7 44.♗b3 ♖e7 45.♖e3
♖c6 46.♔d2 ♖b6 47.♖e4 ♘f6
48.♖c4 ♔b7 49.♖d3 ♖c7 50.♖c7
♔c7 51.♔c3 ♘e4 52.♔c4 ♖d6
53.♖d6 ♔d6 54.♔d3 ♘f2 55.♔e2
♘g4 56.h3 ♘f6 57.♗c4 e4 58.♔e3
♔e5 59.g4 ♘d7 60.♗a6 ♘b6
61.♗b7 ♘c4 62.♔e2 ♔f4, 1-0

Game 149
Pytel,K—Gralka,J
Poland 1979

1.d4 d5 2.c4 e6 3.♘c3 c6 4.♘f3
♘f6 5.e3 ♘bd7 6.♗d3 dc4 7.♗c4
b5 8.♗e2 a6 9.e4 b4 10.e5 bc3
11.ef6 cb2 12.fg7 ♗g7 13.♗b2 ♕a5

14.♘d2 ♖b8 15.♕c2 0-0 16.0-0 c5 17.♘b3 ♕a4 18.dc5 ♗b2 19.♕b2 ♘c5 20.♕e5 ♘d7 21.♕g5 ♔h8 22.♘c5 ♕a5 23.♖ac1 ♗g8 24.♕f4 ♕d8 25.♘d7 ♗d7 26.♖fd1 f6 27.♖c7 ♖g7 28.♕d6 ♕g8 29.g3 ♗b5 30.♖g7 ♔g7 31.♗h5 ♖b7 32.♖d4 f5 33.♕e5 ♔h6 34.♕f6, 1-0

Game 150
Shneider—Kishnev,S
Samarkand 1983

1.d4 d5 2.c4 e6 3.♘c3 c6 4.♘f3 ♘f6 5.e3 ♘bd7 6.♗d3 dc4 7.♗c4 b5 8.♗e2 a6 9.e4 b4 10.e5 bc3 11.ef6 cb2 12.fg7 ♗g7 13.♗b2 ♕a5 14.♘d2 ♖b8 15.♕c1 ♕g5 16.0-0 c5 17.♘b3 ♕c1 18.♖ac1 ♗b7 19.♗a3 cd4 20.♗d6 ♖d8 21.♖c7 ♗d5 22.♗a6 ♗e5 23.♗e5 ♘e5 24.♖e1 d3 25.♘d2 ♘g6 26.♗d3 ♗a2 27.♗b5 ♔f8 28.♘e4 h6 29.♖a1 ♗d5 30.♘f6 ♔g7 31.♘h5 ♔f8 32.f4 ♘h4 33.♖aa7 ♖h7 34.♗d3 ♘f5 35.♗f5 ef5 36.♘f6 ♖h8 37.♘d5 ♖d5 38.♖f7 ♔e8 39.♖fb7 ♖d1 40.♔f2 ♖d2 41.♔e3 ♖d8 42.♖e7 ♔f8 43.♖f7 ♔g8 44.♖f5 h5 45.♖aa5, 1-0

Game 151
Ilincic,Z—Kosic,D
Yugoslavia 1995

1.d4 d5 2.c4 e6 3.♘c3 c6 4.♘f3 ♘f6 5.e3 ♘bd7 6.♗d3 dc4 7.♗c4 b5 8.♗e2 a6 9.e4 b4 10.e5 bc3 11.ef6 cb2 12.fg7 ♗g7 13.♗b2 ♕a5

14.♘d2 ♕g5 15.♗f1 a5 16.♕f3 ♗b7 17.♗d3 0-0 18.h4 ♕f6 19.♕f6 ♘f6 20.♖c1 ♖fd8 21.♖h3 ♘h5 22.♖c5 ♘f4 23.♖g3 ♗a6 24.♗c4 ♗c4 25.♘c4 ♖d5 26.♖c6 ♖ad8 27.♗c3 ♔h8 28.♘e3 ♖h5 29.♖g4 ♘d3 30.♔f1 ♖b5 31.♖c7 h5 32.♖g5 ♖g5 33.hg5 ♔g8 34.♖a7 ♗d4 35.♗d4 ♖d4 36.♖a5 ♔g7 37.♖a7 ♔g6 38.a4 ♘c5 39.a5 ♖a4 40.f3 ♔g3 41.♔f2 ♘b3 42.♖b7 ♘a5 43.♖a7 ♖a2 44.♔g3 ♖e2 45.♘f5 ef 46.♖a5 f4 47.♔f4 ♖g2 48.♖a6, 1/2-1/2

Game 152
Sadler,M—Kaidanov,G
Andorra 1991

1.d4 d5 2.c4 e6 3.♘c3 c6 4.e3 ♘f6 5.♘f3 ♘bd7 6.♗d3 dc4 7.♗c4 b5 8.♗e2 ♗b7 9.e4 b4 10.e5 bc3 11.ef6 cb2 12.fg7 ba1=♕ 13.gh8=♕

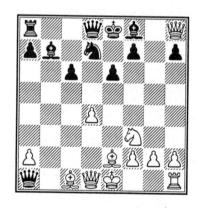

13...♕a5 14.♘d2 ♕f5 15.0-0 0-0-0 16.♕b3 ♘c5 17.♕b4 ♕c2 18.♕f6 ♕cc3 19.♕c3 ♕c3 20.♘f3 ♘e4

21.♕f7 c5 22.♗f4 ♗d6 23.♕e6
♔b8 24.♗d6 ♘d6 25.♕e7 ♕a5
26.dc5 ♘c8 27.♕e5 ♕c7 28.♕c7
♔c7 29.♖d1 ♖e8 30.♗b5 ♖g8
31.♖d7 ♔b8 32.c6 ♗a8 33.♘e5 a5
34.♖h7, 1-0

Queen's Gambit [D53]

Game 153
Ree,H—Borsna
Netherlands 1985

1.c4 e6 2.♘f3 d5 3.d4 ♘f6 4.♗g5
♗e7 5.♘c3 0-0 6.♕c2 h6 7.♗f6
♗f6 8.0-0-0 c5 9.dc5 d4 10.e3 dc3
11.♖d8 cb2

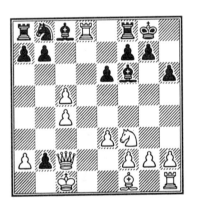

12.♔b1 ♖d8 13.♘d2 g6 14.♘e4
♗g7 15.♘c3 ♘a6 16.♘a4 ♘b4
17.♕e2 ♗d7 18.♘b2 ♗c6 19.f3 b6
20.a3 bc5 21.ab4 cb4 22.♘d3 a5
23.g3 a4 24.♗g2 a3 25.♔a2 b3
26.♔b3 a2 27.e4 ♖db8 28.♔c2
♗a4 29.♔d2 ♖b1, 0-1

Queen's Gambit [D60]

Game 154
Novikov,I—Kazautzev
Perm 1986

1.d4 d5 2.c4 e6 3.♘c3 ♘f6 4.♗g5
♗e7 5.e3 0-0 6.♘f3 ♘bd7 7.♗d3
c5 8.cd5 cd4 9.de6 dc3 10.ed7 cb2
11.dc8=♕ ba1=♕

12.♗h7, 1-0

Game 155
Benderac,A—Peres,T
Mamaia 1991

1.d4 d5 2.c4 e6 3.♘c3 ♘f6 4.♗g5
♘bd7 5.♘f3 ♗e7 6.e3 0-0 7.♗d3
h6 8.♗h4 c5 9.cd5 cd4 10.de6 dc3
11.ed7 cb2 12.dc8=♕

(see next diagram)

12...♕d3 13.♕b7 ♕d1 14.♖d1
♖ab8 15.♕e7 b1=♕ 16.♖b1 ♖b1
17.♔e2 ♖h1 18.♗f6 gf6 19.♕f6
♖b1 20.♘d4 ♖b2 21.♔f3, 1-0

After 12.dc8=♕

11.♗g2 ♗g2 −+ (Black has an extra piece. Surprisingly enough, however, Bogoljubow managed to lose this game) 12.♖g1 ♗b7 13.♗h4 d6 14.e4 ♘bd7 15.♕f3 ♕e7 16.♖g4 e5 17.d5 0-0-0 18.♔e2 ♖dg8 19.♖ag1 ♖g4 20.♖g4 h5 21.♖g3 ♔b8 22.♕f5 ♗c8 23.♗g5 h4 24.♖f3 ♕f8 25.♗f6 ♘f6 26.♕f6 ♗g4 27.h3 ♕h6 28.hg4, 1-0

Queen's Indian Defense [E12]

Game 156
Tarrasch,S—Bogoljubow,E
Goteborg 1920

1.d4 ♘f6 2.♘f3 e6 3.c4 b6 4.♗g5 ♗b7 5.e3 h6 6.♗h4 ♗b4 7.♘bd2 g5 (A case of the Steeplechase as punishment for the premature pinning 4.♗g5) 8.♗g3 g4 9.a3 gf3 10.ab4 fg2

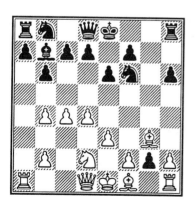

Queen's Indian Defense [E17]

Game 157
Dalmagro,D—Zalisnak,J
Saladillo 1992

1.d4 e6 2.♘f3 ♘f6 3.c4 b6 4.g3 ♗b7 5.♗g2 ♗e7 6.0-0 0-0 7.♘c3 d5 8.b3 ♘bd7 9.♗b2 ♖c8 10.♘e5 c5 11.cd5 cd4 12.♘f7 ♔f7 13.de6 ♔e6 14.♗b7 dc3 15.♗c8

15...cb2 16.♗d7 ♕d7 17.♖b1 ♕d1 18.♖fd1 ♗a3 19.b4 ♖c8 20.e4 ♘e4

21.♖e1 ♖c1 22.f3 ♖b1 23.♖b1 ♘c3
24.♖e1 ♔f7, 0-1

Old Indian Defense [E97]

Game 158
Gavrikov, V—Saitzev
Pardulice 1997

1.d4 ♘f6 2.c4 g6 3.♘c3 ♗g7 4.e4
d6 5.♘f3 0-0 6.♗e2 e5 7.0-0 ♘c6
8.d5 ♘e7 9.b4 ♘h5 10.♖e1 ♘f4
11.♗f1 h6 12.c5 f5 13.♗f4 fe4
14.♗e5 ef3 15.♗g7 fg2 16.♗f8
gf1=♕

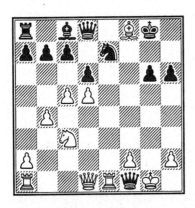

17.♖f1 ♕f8 18.cd6 cd6 19.f3 ♗h3
20.♖f2 ♕f5 21.♕d4 ♖f8 22.♕h4
♕e5 23.♕h3 ♕c3 24.♕e6 ♖f7
25.♖b1 ♘f5 26.♔h1 ♔g7 27.♖g1
g5 28.♕e4 ♕f6 29.h4 ♕g6 30.hg5
♘g3 31.♖g3 ♕e4 32.gh6 ♔h7
33.♖g7 ♔h6 34.fe4 ♖f2 35.♖d7
♖a2 36.♖d6 ♔g5 37.♖e6 ♔f4 38.d6
a5 39.ba5 ♖a5 40.e5 ♖d5 41.♖e7
♔g3 42.♖g7 ♔f4 43.d7 ♖d1
44.♔g2, 0-1

Part Three

The Middlegame Steeplechase

The a-pawn March

Game 159
Steinitz,W—Martinez,J
Philadelphia 1882

1.e4 e5 2.f4 &c5 3.&f3 d6 4.c3 &g4
5.&c4 &f6 6.fe5 &f3 7.&f3 de5
8.d3 &bd7 9.b4 &b6 10.a4 a5
11.g4 h6 12.b5 &e7 13.&d2 0-0-0
14.&b3 &b8 15.&a3 &c5 16.&c5
&c5 17.&a5 h5 18.g5 &g4 19.&b3
&a7 20.h4 f6 21.gf6 gf6 22.a5 &d6
23.a6 &e3 24.ab7

24...&c2 25.&e2 &a1 26.&a1 f5
27.ef5 &h4 28.&d5 e4 29.&e4 &g8
30.&h1 &f6 31.&d2 &e5 32.&c2
&b5 33.&h5 &gd8 34.&h1 &b6

35.&b1 &h8 36.&e2 &a4 37.d4
&e8 38.&f3 &h6 39.&a1 &c4
40.&c5 &f7 41.&a6 &d6 42.&d6
&a2 43.&d3 &b1 44.&c4, 1-0

Game 160
Timman,J—Yusupov,A
Tilburg 1986

1.d4 d5 2.c4 e6 3.&c3 &f6 4.&f3
&e7 5.&g5 h6 6.&f6 &f6 7.&b3 c6
8.0-0-0 dc4 9.&c4 b5 10.&b3 a5
11.e4 a4 12.&c2 &d7 13.d5 cd5
14.ed5 a3 15.de6 ab2

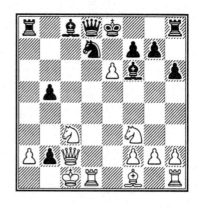

16.&b1 fe6 17.&e4 &c3 18.&a8
0-0 19.&c6 b4 20.&c4 &h8
21.&e4 &c7 22.&h4 &e5 23.&d3
&d3 24.&g6 &g8 25.&d3 &f2
26.&f3 &f3 27.gf3 &d6 28.&c2 e5
29.&h4 &e6 30.&d1 &d5 31.&a4
&d8 32.&c6 &d4 33.&d4 ed4
34.&b5 &a8 35.&b2 &a2 36.&c1
&a1 37.&d2 &c3 38.&d1 &b3,
0-1

Game 161
Gleizerov,E—Dvoirys,S
Cheljabinsk 1990

1.d4 ♘f6 2.c4 c5 3.♘f3 cd4 4.♘d4
♘c6 5.♘c3 e6 6.g3 ♕b6 7.♘b3
♘e5 8.e4 ♗b4 9.♕e2 d6 10.♗d2
0-0 11.0-0-0 a5 12.f4 ♘c6 13.♗e3
♕a6 14.♘b5 a4 15.♘c7 ab3
16.♘a6 ba2

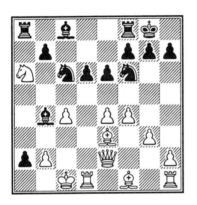

17.♔c2 ♖a6 18.♗g2 e5 19.f5 ♗c5
20.b3 ♗d7 21.♔b2 ♘d4 22.♗d4
a1=♕ 23.♖a1 ♗d4 24.♔c2 ♗a1,
0-1

Game 162
De Firmian,N—Shirov,A
Biel 1995

1.e4 c5 2.♘f3 d6 3.d4 cd4 4.♘d4
♘c6 5.♘c3 ♘f6 6.♗c4 e6 7.♗e3
♗e7 8.♗b3 a6 9.♕e2 ♕c7 10.0-0-0
0-0 11.g4 ♘d4 12.♖d4 ♘d7 13.g5
♘c5 14.♖g1 b5 15.♕h5 g6 16.♕h6
♖d8 17.e5 ♗f8 18.♕h3 ♗g7
19.♖d6 ♗b7 20.♗f4 ♖d6 21.ed6
♕c6 22.♖d1 b4 23.♘e2 a5 24.♗c4

a4 25.♕e3 b3 26.♘c3 a3 27.♗e5
ab2

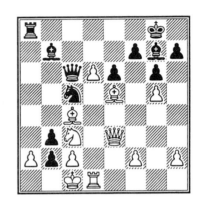

28.♔b2 ♘a4 29.♘a4 bc2 30.♖d4
♗e5 31.♕e5 ♖a4 32.d7 c1=♕
33.♔c1 ♖c4 34.♖c4 ♕c4 35.♔b2
♕b4 36.♔c1 ♕a3 37.♕b2 ♕c5
38.♔b1 ♗e4 39.♔a1 ♕d6 40.♕b5
♕d4, 0-1

The b-pawn March

Game 163
Verlinsky,B—Riumin
Moscow 1933

1.e4 c5 2.♘f3 ♘c6 3.d4 cd4 4.♘d4
♘f6 5.♘c3 d6 6.♗e2 g6 7.♗e3
♗g7 8.♕d2 0-0 9.♘b3 a6 10.f3
♗e6 11.g4 b5 12.g5 ♘d7 13.h4
b4 14.♘a4 ♕c7 15.0-0-0 ♖fd8
16.♕e1 ♘a5 17.♔b1 ♖dc8 18.♖c1
♘c4 19.♗c4 ♕c4 20.♕f2 ♕b5
21.♘b6 ♘b6 22.♗b6 a5 23.♗d4 a4
24.♘d2 b3 25.♗g7 bc2

(see next diagram)

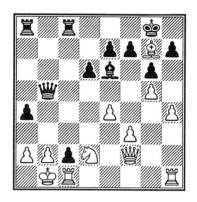

26.♔a1 ♚g7 27.a3 ♛d3 28.♖he1
♖c3 29.b3 ♖b3 30.♘b3 ♛c3
31.♔a2 ab3#, 0-1

Game 164
Novosibirsk—Saratov
1960

1.d4 ♘f6 2.c4 g6 3.♘c3 ♝g7 4.e4
d6 5.f3 0-0 6.♘ge2 ♘bd7 7.♝e3 e5
8.♛d2 c6 9.d5 cd5 10.cd5 a6
11.0-0-0 b5 12.♔b1 ♘b6 13.♘c1
b4 14.♝b6 bc3 15.♛e3 ♖b8
16.♝d8 ♖b2 17.♔a1 c2 18.♘b3
cd1=♛

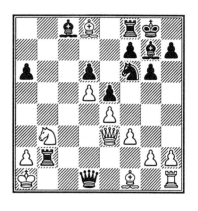

19.♔b2 ♖d8 20.♖g1 ♘d5 21.ed5
♛d5 22.♛b6 ♖e8, 0-1

Game 165
Westerinin,H—Westmann
Upsala 1966

1.e4 c5 2.♘f3 d6 3.d4 cd4 4.♘d4
♘f6 5.♘c3 a6 6.♝g5 e6 7.♝e2 ♝e7
8.0-0 0-0 9.f4 ♛c7 10.♔h1 ♝d7
11.♝f3 ♘c6 12.♘b3 ♖ac8 13.♖e1
h6 14.♝f6 ♝f6 15.♛d2 b5 16.♖ad1
b4 17.♛d6 bc3 18.e5 cb2 19.♛d7
b1=♛

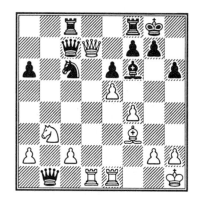

20.♛c7 ♛d1 21.♖d1 ♖c7 22.ef6
♘b4 23.fg7 ♔g7 24.♖d4 ♖b8 25.c4
♘a2 26.♝d1 ♖b4, 0-1

Game 166
Mestel,J—Pasman,M
Beersheba 1984

1.c4 ♘f6 2.g3 c6 3.♘f3 d5 4.b3 ♝f5
5.♝b2 e6 6.♝g2 h6 7.0-0 ♝e7 8.d3
0-0 9.♘bd2 a5 10.a3 ♝h7 11.♛c2
♘bd7 12.♖fc1 ♛b8 13.♛c3 b5
14.♘d4 b4 15.♛c2 ♛b6 16.cd5 cd5
17.♛c6 ba3 18.♛b6 ab2

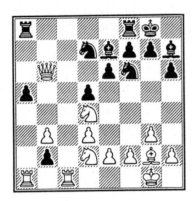

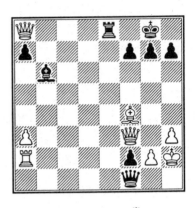

After 21.ba8=♕

19.♕c6 ♗c5 20.♕a4 ♖fc8 21.♘c6
♖c7 22.b4 ♗d4 23.♖ab1 ♘b6
24.♕b5 bc1=♕ 25.♖c1 ♘g4
26.ba5 ♗f2 27.♔f1 ♘c8 28.♗f3
♗e3 29.♗g4 ♗d2 30.♖b1 ♗e3
31.a6 ♗g6 32.♕b7 ♖b7 33.ab7, 1-0

Game 167
Gavrikov, V—Kharitonov, A
Moscow 1988

1.d4 ♘f6 2.c4 e6 3.♘f3 d5 4.♘c3
♗e7 5.♗f4 0-0 6.e3 c5 7.dc5 ♗c5
8.cd5 ♘d5 9.♘d5 ed5 10.a3 ♘c6
11.♗d3 ♗b6 12.0-0 ♗g4 13.h3
♗h5 14.b4 ♖e8 15.♖a2 d4 16.b5
♗f3 17.♕f3 de3 18.bc6 ♕d3
19.cb7 ef2 20.♔h2 ♕f1 21.ba8=♕

(see next diagram)

21...♕g1 22.♔g3 f1=♘ 23.♔h4
♗d8 24.♕d8 ♖d8 25.♖f2 f6 26.♖f1
g5 27.♔h5 ♕c5 28.♗e3 ♕c4
29.♔h6 ♖e8 30.♗d2 ♕f7 31.♕d3
♖e2 32.♕d8 ♖e8 33.♕d3 ♖e2
34.♕d8 ♖e8 35.♕d3, 1/2-1/2

Game 168
Serper, G—Gelman
Reno 1996

1.c4 e5 2.♘c3 ♘c6 3.g3 g6 4.♗g2
♗g7 5.♖b1 d6 6.b4 a6 7.d3 f5
8.e3 e4 9.♘d5 ♘e5 10.de4 fe4
11.♗e4 c6 12.♘f4 ♘c4 13.♘ge2 d5
14.♗g2 a5 15.b5 ♗f5 16.bc6 ♗b1
17.cb7

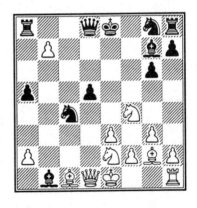

17...♖b8 18.♗d5 ♘e5 19.♕b3 ♗f5
20.♗g8 g5 21.♘d4 a4 22.♕a4 ♗d7
23.♕b3 gf4 24.gf4 ♘d3 25.♔d2

♕e7 26.♗a3 ♖b7 27.♕d3 ♖b4 28.♖b1 ♖b1 29.♗e7 ♖b2 30.♔c1 ♖f2 31.♕c4 ♔e7 32.♕f7 ♔d6 33.♕g7 ♖h2 34.♕e5#, 1-0

The c-pawn March

Game 169
Riemann,F—Tarrasch,S
Hamburg 1885

1.e4 e6 2.d4 d5 3.♘c3 ♘f6 4.♗g5 ♗e7 5.♗f6 ♗f6 6.♘f3 0-0 7.e5 ♗e7 8.♗d3 f6 9.♘e2 c5 10.c3 fe5 11.de5 ♘c6 12.♘g3 ♗d7 13.♕b1 ♕c7 14.♗h7 ♔h8 15.h4 ♘e5 16.♘g5 c4 17.♕d1 ♖f6 18.f4 ♘c6 19.♗c2 ♗e8 20.♘e2 ♗d6 21.g3 ♕b6 22.b3 ♗h5 23.bc4 dc4 24.♖b1 ♕c7 25.♘e4 ♖d8 26.♘f6 gf6 27.♕c1 ♗c5 28.f5 ♕g7 29.♕f4 ♘e5 30.♖f1 ♘d3 31.♗d3 cd3 32.g4 de2 33.gh5 ef1=♕

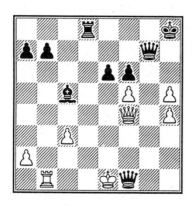

34.♔f1 ♖d3 35.♕b8 ♕g8 36.♖b7 ♖d8 37.♕h2 ♕g4, 0-1

Game 170
Pillsbury,H—Marco,G
Hamburg 1885

1.d4 d5 2.c4 e6 3.♘c3 ♘f6 4.♘f3 ♗e7 5.♗f4 0-0 6.♖c1 c6 7.e3 b6 8.♗d3 ♗b7 9.0-0 ♘bd7 10.e4 de4 11.♘e4 ♘e4 12.♗e4 ♘f6 13.♗b1 c5 14.dc5 ♕d1 15.♖fd1 ♗c5 16.a3 ♖fd8 17.b4 ♗e7 18.♘d4 ♘e8 19.♗a2 a5 20.c5 ab4 21.c6 ♗c8 22.c7

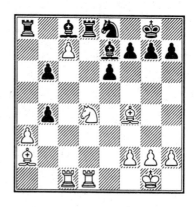

22...♖d7 23.♘c6 ♗f6 24.♘b4 ♖d1 25.♖d1 ♗b7 26.♖d7 ♔f8 27.♗c4 ♗e7 28.h3 ♖c8 29.♗a6 ♗a6 30.♘a6 ♘f6 31.♖d3 ♘d5 32.♗e3 ♔e8, 0-1

Game 171
Lasker,Em—Alekhine,A
St. Petersburg 1914

1.d4 d5 2.c4 e5 3.de5 d4 4.♘f3 ♘c6 5.a3 ♗g4 6.♘bd2 ♕e7 7.h3 ♗f3 8.♘f3 0-0-0 9.♕d3 h6 10.g3 g6 11.♗g2 ♗g7 12.0-0 ♘e5 13.♘e5

♗e5 14.b4 f5 15.c5 ♕e6 16.c6 ♘e7
17.cb7

17...♔b8 18.♗b2 ♖d6 19.♖ac1
♖hd8 20.♖c2 f4 21.gf4 ♗f4 22.♖d1
♘f5 23.♗c1 ♘e3 24.♖c5 ♕f6
25.♕e4 ♘d1 26.♗f4 ♘c3 27.♗d6
♕d6 28.♕e5 ♕b6 29.♕e7 ♕d6
30.♖e5 d3 31.ed3 ♕d3 32.♖e3
♕d1 33.♔h2 ♘b5 34.♖e6 ♘a3
35.♖f6, 1-0

Game 172
Aisenstadt—Taimanov,M
Leningrad 1949

1.d4 d5 2.c4 e6 3.♘f3 ♘f6 4.g3 dc4
5.♗g2 ♘c6 6.♕a4 ♗b4 7.♗d2
♘d5 8.♗b4 ♘db4 9.a3 b5 10.♕b5
♘c2 11.♔d2 ♘a1 12.♕c6 ♗d7
13.♕c4 ♖b8 14.b4 c5 15.♘c3 cd4
16.♘e4 ♗b5 17.♕a2 d3 18.♕a1 de2

(see next diagram)

19.♕d4 0-0 20.♘d6 ♗a6 21.♖c1
♖b6 22.♘c4 ♗c4 23.♖c4 ♖d6
24.♔e2 ♖d4 25.♘d4 ♕b6, 0-1

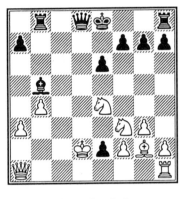

After 18...de2

Game 173
Tal,M—Portisch,L
Bled 1965

1.e4 c6 2.♘c3 d5 3.♘f3 de4 4.♘e4
♗g4 5.h3 ♗f3 6.♕f3 ♘d7 7.d4
♘gf6 8.♗d3 ♘e4 9.♕e4 e6 10.0-0
♗e7 11.c3 ♘f6 12.♕h4 ♘d5
13.♕g4 ♗f6 14.♖e1 ♕b6 15.c4
♘b4 16.♖e6 fe6 17.♕e6 ♔f8
18.♗f4 ♖d8 19.c5 ♘d3 20.cb6 ♘f4
21.♕g4 ♘d5 22.ba7

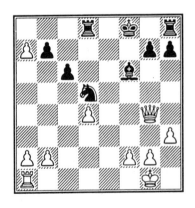

22...♔e7 23.b4 ♖a8 24.♖e1 ♔d6
25.b5 ♖a7 26.♖e6 ♔c7 27.♖f6, 1-0

Game 174
Tukmakov,V—Kherkin
Iraklion 1992

1.d4 d5 2.c4 c6 3.♘f3 ♘f6 4.♘c3
e6 5.♗g5 dc4 6.e4 b5 7.e5 h6
8.♗h4 g5 9.ef6 gh4 10.♘e5 ♕f6
11.a4 h3 12.g3 c5 13.♗h3 cd4
14.♘g4 ♕g7 15.♕f3 dc3 16.♕a8
cb2

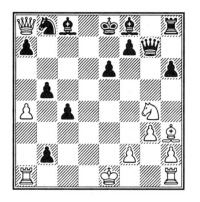

17.♖d1 ♗b4 18.♔e2 c3 19.♕b8 0-0
20.♕b5 c2 21.♕b4 ♗a6 22.♔e3
♖c8 23.♖c1 h5 24.♔d2 ♕g5
25.♘e3 ♕d8, 0-1

Game 175
Filippov—Fritz 3
Moscow 1996

1.c4 ♘f6 2.♘c3 c5 3.g3 e6 4.♗g2
d5 5.e3 dc4 6.♕a4 ♘c6 7.♗c6 bc6
8.♕c6 ♗d7 9.♕a6 ♗e7 10.♘ge2
0-0 11.0-0 e5 12.♕c4 ♗e6 13.♕a4
♕d3 14.♕b5 ♗c4 15.♕b7 ♗d6
16.b3 ♗a6 17.♕g2 ♖ab8 18.♗a3

♖fd8 19.♖fd1 ♗e7 20.♖ac1 ♗d6
21.g4 c4 22.♗d6 ♖d6 23.g5 ♘d7
24.♘e4 ♖db6 25.♘4g3 cb3 26.♖c3
ba2

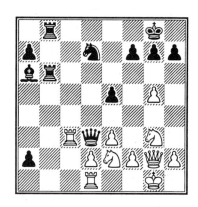

27.♖d3 ♖b1 28.♘c3 ♗d3 29.♕f3
e4, 0-1

Game 176
Ristic—Savanovic,A
Yugoslavia 1997

1.d4 d5 2.c4 c6 3.♘f3 ♘f6 4.♘c3 e6
5.♗g5 dc4 6.e4 b5 7.a4 ♗b4 8.e5
h6 9.♗h4 g5 10.ef6 gh4 11.♘e5
♗b7 12.♗e2 c5 13.♗f3 ♗f3 14.♕f3
cd4 15.♕a8 dc3 16.0-0 cb2

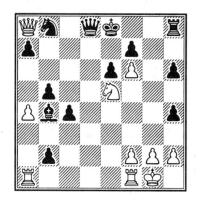

17.♖ad1 ♕c7 18.♘c6 ♗d6 19.♘b8
0-0 20.♕f3 ♖b8 21.g4 ♔f8 22.♖fe1
♖b6 23.a5 ♖c6 24.♕h4 c3 25.♕h6
♔e8 26.♕h5 c2 27.♖e6 ♔d7
28.♖e7 ♔c8 29.♕f5 ♔d8 30.♖de1
♗e7 31.fe7 ♕e7 32.♕d5 ♕d7
33.♕g5 ♔c8 34.♕g8 ♔b7 35.a6
♔a6, 0-1

Game 177
Ivanchuk, V—Georgiev, K
Belgrade 1997

1.c4 c5 2.♘f3 g6 3.d4 cd4 4.♘d4
♘c6 5.e4 ♘f6 6.♘c3 d6 7.f3 ♘d4
8.♕d4 ♗g7 9.♗e3 0-0 10.♕d2
♗e6 11.♖c1 ♕a5 12.b3 ♖fc8
13.♗e2 a6 14.♘a4 ♕d2 15.♔d2
♘d7 16.g4 f5 17.ef5 gf5 18.h3 ♖f8
19.f4 ♘f6 20.♖hg1 ♖ad8 21.♗b6
♖c8 22.♘c3 ♖c6 23.♗e3 fg4
24.hg4 d5 25.f5 ♖d8 26.♔e1 d4
27.♖d1 ♖cd6 28.c5 ♘d5 29.cd6
♘e3 30.de7

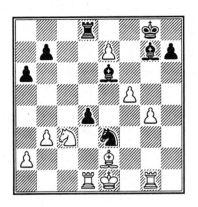

30...♖e8 31.fe6 ♖e7 32.♘e4, 1-0

Game 178
Van Wely, L—Topalov, V
Wijk ann Zee 1998

1.d4 ♘f6 2.c4 e6 3.♘f3 c5 4.d5 d6
5.♘c3 ed5 6.cd5 g6 7.h3 ♗g7 8.e4
0-0 9.♗d3 b5 10.♘b5 ♖e8 11.♘d2
♘e4 12.♗e4 ♗a6 13.a4 ♕a5
14.♘d6 ♘d7 15.♕c2 f5 16.♘e8
♖e8 17.♔d1 fe4 18.♖a3 c4 19.♖e3
♕d5 20.♖e4 ♖f8 21.f3 ♘c5 22.♖e7
♗f6 23.♖a7 c3 24.♖a6 cd2 25.♖f6
dc1=♕

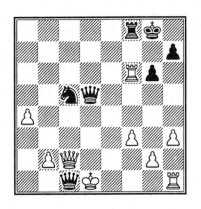

26.♔c1 ♖f6 27.♖d1 ♕c6 28.♔b1
♘a4 29.♕c6 ♖c6 30.♖d8 ♔g7
31.♖d7 ♔h6 32.h4 ♘c5 33.♖f7 ♘e6
34.♔a2 ♖a6 35.♔b1 ♘d4 36.♖f4
♘f5 37.♖e4 ♖d6 38.♔c2 ♘g3
39.♖g4 ♘f1 40.♔c3 ♘e3 41.♖g5
♘f5 42.♖g4 ♔h5 43.b4 ♘e3 44.♖d4
♖d4 45.♔d4 ♘c2 46.♔e5 ♘b4
47.♔f6 ♘d5 48.♔g7 ♘e3, 0-1

The d-pawn March

Game 179
Neumann,G—Anderssen,A
Berlin 1866

1.d4 f5 2.e4 fe4 3.♘c3 ♘f6 4.♗g5 c6 5.♗f6 ef6 6.♘e4 d5 7.♘g3 ♗d6 8.♗d3 0-0 9.♕h5 g6 10.♕h6 ♖f7 11.♘1e2 ♘d7 12.h4 ♘f8 13.f4 ♕e7 14.♔d2 ♗g4 15.♖ae1 ♖e8 16.f5 ♗g3 17.♘g3 ♕b4 18.c3 ♕b2 19.♗c2 ♖fe7 20.♖e7 ♖e7 21.h5 ♗f5 22.♘f5 gf5 23.g4 ♖e4 24.♖f1 ♖g4 25.♕e3 c5 26.♖g1 ♖g1 27.♕g1 ♔f7 28.dc5 ♘e6 29.c6 d4 30.cb7

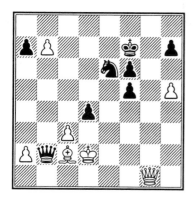

30...dc3 31.♔d3 ♘f4 32.♔c4 ♕b7 33.♗b3 ♕c7 34.♔b4 ♘e6 35.h6 ♕b6 36.♕b6 ab6 37.♔c3 f4 38.♗c2 ♘g5 39.♗f5 ♔e7 40.♔d4 ♔d6 41.♗c2 ♔e6 42.♗d3 f5 43.♗c4 ♔d6 44.♗g8 f3 45.♗c4 f4 46.♗f1 f2 47.♔d3 ♔e5 48.♔e2 ♘e4 49.♗g2 ♔f5 50.a3 f3 51.♗f3 f1=♕ 52.♔f1 ♘d2 53.♔f2 ♘f3 54.♔f3 ♔g5, 0-1

Game 180
Zuckermann,B—Tartakower,S
Paris 1930

1.d4 ♘f6 2.♘f3 b6 3.c4 ♗b7 4.g3 c5 5.d5 e6 6.♘c3 ed5 7.cd5 b5 8.♗g5 b4 9.♘e4 d6 10.♗f6 gf6 11.♕a4 ♔e7 12.♘h4 ♗c8 13.♗g2 ♕b6 14.♖c1 ♘a6 15.♕b3 ♗h6 16.♕f3 f5 17.♖c4 fe4 18.♖e4 ♔f8 19.♕f6 ♗g7 20.♕e7 ♔g8 21.♕e8 ♗f8 22.♖e7 ♗e6 23.de6 ♖e8 24.ef7 ♔g7 25.fe8=♕, 1-0

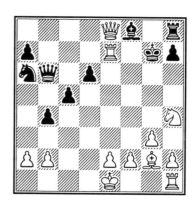

final position

Game 181
Panov,V—Sorokin,N
USSR 1953

1.e4 c5 2.♘f3 d6 3.d4 cd4 4.♘d4 ♘f6 5.♘c3 a6 6.g3 ♗g4 7.f3 ♗d7 8.♗e3 ♘c6 9.♕d2 g6 10.♘d5 ♘d5 11.ed5 ♘e5 12.h3 ♗c8 13.f4 ♘d7 14.♗g2 ♗g7 15.0-0 0-0 16.♖ad1 a5 17.♔h2 ♘c5 18.f5 ♗d7 19.♗h6 ♕b6 20.b3 ♕b4 21.♕e3 ♖ae8 22.♗g7 ♔g7 23.♖f4 ♕b6 24.♖h4

h5 25.♕g5 ♖h8 26.♖e1 ♕d8
27.♘e6 (Alekhine's Block!) 27...♗e6
28.de6 ♖h6 29.ef7

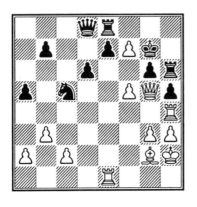

29...♖f8 30.♖h5 ♖fh8 31.♖e7 ♘d7
32.♖h6 ♖h6 33.f6, 1-0

Game 182
Katalymov,B—Muratov,V
Alma Ata 1961

1.b4 e6 2.♗b2 ♘f6 3.a3 d5 4.e3
♗e7 5.c4 dc4 6.♗c4 0-0 7.♘f3
♘bd7 8.♕c2 ♘b6 9.♗e2 ♗d7
10.♘c3 ♘fd5 11.♘d5 ♘d5 12.♗d3
h6 13.h4 a6 14.g4 ♗f6 15.♘e5
♗b5 16.♗h7 ♔h8 17.g5 ♗e5
18.♗e5 f5 19.gf6 gf6 20.♗b2 a5
21.ba5 ♕d7 22.♗g6 ♖a5 23.♕c5
♖g8 24.♖g1 e5 25.d4 b6 26.de5
bc5 27.ef6 ♖g6 28.f7 ♔h7 29.f8=♘

(see next diagram)

29...♔g8 30.♘g6 ♕d6 31.0-0-0
♔f7 32.e4 ♘f4 33.♖d6 ♘e2
34.♔d2 cd6 35.♘h8 ♔e7 36.♖g7
♔d8 37.♘f7 ♔c7 38.♘h6 ♔c6

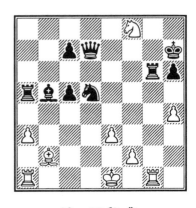

After 29.f8=♘

39.♘f7 c4 40.♘d8 ♔b6 41.♖b7
♔a6 42.♔e2 c3 43.♖b5 ♔b5
44.♗c3, 1-0

Game 183
Tal,M—Padevsky,N
Moscow 1963

1.e4 e6 2.d4 d5 3.♘c3 ♗b4 4.e5
b6 5.♕g4 ♗f8 6.♗g5 ♕d7 7.♘f3
♘c6 8.a3 ♗b7 9.♗d3 h6 10.♗d2
0-0-0 11.h4 ♘ge7 12.0-0-0 f5
13.ef6 gf6 14.♖de1 ♖g8 15.♕e6
♖g2 16.♕e3 ♔b8 17.♗f1 ♖g8
18.♗h3 f5 19.♕d3 ♗c8 20.h5 ♕e8
21.♗f4 ♕h5 22.♘b5 ♖d7 23.♕c3
♗b7 24.♘e5 ♘e5 25.de5 d4 26.e6
dc3 27.ed7

(see next diagram)

27...♗g7 28.♘c7, 1-0

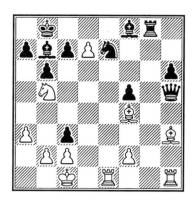

After 27.ed7

Game 184
Bilek,I—Tal,M
Moscow 1967

1.♘f3 ♘f6 2.g3 b5 3.♗g2 ♗b7
4.0-0 e6 5.d3 d5 6.♘bd2 ♗e7 7.e4
0-0 8.♕e2 c5 9.♖e1 ♘c6 10.c3 a5
11.ed5 ed5 12.d4 ♕b6 13.dc5 ♗c5
14.♘b3 ♖fe8 15.♕c2 d4 16.♕f5
♖e1 17.♘e1 ♖e8 18.♘f3 ♗d6
19.♗g5 ♘e4 20.♖e1 ♘e7 21.♗e7
g6 22.♕h3 dc3 23.♖e4 cb2

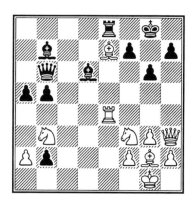

24.♖e1 ♖e7 25.♖b1 a4 26.♘bd4
♗f3 27.♘f3 ♖e2 28.♖f1 ♖f2
29.♕c8 ♔g7 30.♕c3 f6, 0-1

Game 185
Peev,P—Bogosian
Bulgaria 1968

1.d4 ♘f6 2.c4 c5 3.d5 e5 4.♘c3 d6
5.e4 ♗e7 6.♘ge2 0-0 7.♘g3 ♘e8
8.h4 a6 9.♗d3 ♘d7 10.♘f5 ♘df6
11.g4 ♘c7 12.♕e2 ♔h8 13.♗d2
♖b8 14.0-0-0 b5 15.f4 bc4 16.♗c4
♘d7 17.g5 ef4 18.♗f4 ♘b6 19.♘e7
♕e7 20.e5 ♘c4 21.♕c4 de5 22.d6
♕e6 23.dc7 ♕c4 24.cb8=♕

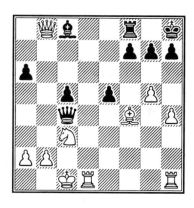

24...♕f4 25.♖d2 ♔g8 26.♕d6 ♗f5
27.♕c5 ♖c8 28.♕f2 ♕e4 29.♖d8
♖d8 30.♘e4, 1-0

Game 186
Jadas—Bozic
corr. 1968

1.e4 e5 2.♘f3 ♘c6 3.♗b5 a6 4.♗a4
♘f6 5.0-0 ♗e7 6.♖e1 b5 7.♗b3 0-0
8.c3 d6 9.h3 h6 10.d4 ♖e8 11.♘bd2
♗f8 12.♘f1 ♗d7 13.♘g3 ♘a5

14.♗c2 ♘c4 15.♗d3 ♘b6 16.♗e3
c5 17.♕e2 ♖c8 18.♖ac1 cd4 19.cd4
♘c4 20.♗c4 bc4 21.d5 a5 22.♖c3
♗b5 23.♕c2 ♖e7 24.a4 ♗a6
25.♘d2 ♖b7 26.b3 ♖b4 27.♘c4
♗c4 28.♖c4 ♖cc4 29.bc4 ♕c7
30.♖c1 ♕d7 31.♖a1 ♕c7 32.c5 dc5
33.♗d2 c4 34.♖c1 c3 35.♕d3 cd2
36.♖c7 ♖d4 37.♕a6 d1=♕

After 12.cb7

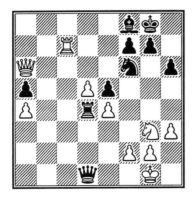

38.♔h2 ♖a4 39.♖c8 ♖a1 40.♖f8
♔h7 41.♘e2 ♘h5 42.♘c1 ♕c1, 0-1

Game 187
Rundau—Schmidt
Germany 1972

1.e4 ♘c6 2.d4 d5 3.ed5 ♕d5 4.♘f3
♗g4 5.♗e2 0-0-0 6.c4 ♕h5 7.d5
♗f3 8.♗f3 ♕e5 9.♗e3 ♕b2 10.0-0
♕a1 11.dc6 ♖d1 12.cb7

(see next diagram)

12...♔b8 13.♖d1 c6 14.♗c6 ♔c7
15.♖d7 ♔c6 16.b8=♘＃, 1-0

Game 188
Sokolov, A—Vekshenkov, N
Novosibirsk 1974

1.♘f3 d5 2.g3 ♗g4 3.♘e5 ♗f5
4.♗g2 ♘d7 5.f4 e6 6.c4 ♘gf6
7.♘c3 d4 8.♗b7 dc3 9.♘c6 c2
10.♘d8 cd1=♕

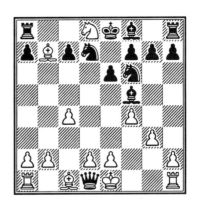

11.♔d1 ♖d8, 0-1

Game 189
Bisguier,A—Karklins,A
Chicago 1974

1.d4 ♘f6 2.c4 e6 3.♘c3 ♗b4 4.♘f3
d6 5.e3 ♘c6 6.♗d2 ♕e7 7.d5 ♗c3
8.♗c3 ♘d8 9.♗d3 e5 10.♕c2 0-0
11.0-0 g6 12.♘d2 ♘h5 13.f4 f5
14.fe5 de5 15.e4 f4 16.b4 ♘f7 17.c5
g5 18.♘c4 g4 19.♖ad1 g3 20.h3
♗h3 21.gh3 ♘g5 22.♘e5 f3 23.♘f3
♖f3 24.♕g2 ♖af8 25.d6 ♕e6
26.dc7

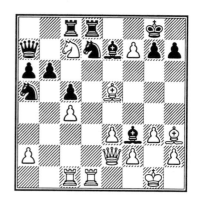

21...♔h8 22.♖d7 ♗e2 23.♖e7 h6
24.♘e8 ♕e7 25.♗g7, 1-0

Game 191
Beliavsky,A—Pinter,J
Trud-Spartakus Match 1984

1.d4 ♘f6 2.c4 e6 3.♘f3 d5 4.♘c3
c6 5.♗g5 dc4 6.e4 b5 7.e5 h6
8.♗h4 g5 9.♘g5 hg5 10.♗g5 ♘bd7
11.ef6 ♗b7 12.g3 c5 13.d5 ♗h6
14.♗h6 ♖h6 15.♕d2 ♖g6 16.0-0-0
♘f6 17.♕e3 ♕b6 18.♗g2 ♔f8
19.♖he1 ♔g8 20.de6 ♗g2 21.ef7

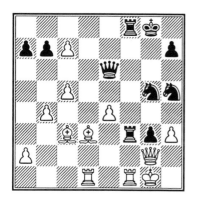

26...♘h3 27.♕h3 ♕h3 28.♗c4, 1-0

Game 190
Moring—Pokoevchik,J
Balatonkerevy 1983

1.♘f3 ♘f6 2.g3 e6 3.c4 d5 4.b3
♗e7 5.♗b2 0-0 6.♗g2 c5 7.0-0
♘c6 8.e3 b6 9.♘c3 dc4 10.bc4
♗b7 11.♕e2 ♖c8 12.♖fd1 ♕c7
13.♖ac1 ♖fd8 14.d4 ♘a5 15.♘b5
♕b8 16.d5 a6 17.♗e5 ♕a8 18.♘c7
♕a7 19.♗h3 ♘d7 20.de6 ♗f3
21.ef7

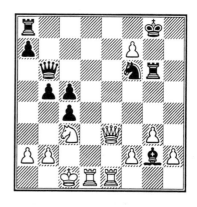

21...♔g7 22.♘e2 c3 23.♘f4 cb2
24.♔b2 ♘e4 25.♘g2 ♕f6 26.♔c2

♕f7 27.♔b1 ♖a6 28.♖e2 ♖e8 29.f3
♘f6 30.♕g5 ♔h7 31.♕f5 ♔g7
32.♖ed2 b4 33.g4 c4 34.♖d7 ♘d7
35.♖d7 ♖e7 36.♕g5 ♔f8 37.♖d8
♖e8 38.♕c5 ♔g8 39.♖e8 ♕e8
40.♕c4 ♕e6 41.♘e3 ♖c6 42.♕b5
♖c3 43.♕b8 ♔f7 44.♕a7 ♔g6
45.♘g2 ♕d6 46.♕g1 b3 47.♕e1
♕d3, 0-1

Game 192
Gavrikov, V—Bagirov, V
Lvov 1984

1.d4 d5 2.c4 c6 3.♘f3 ♘f6 4.♘c3
e6 5.♗g5 dc4 6.e4 b5 7.e5 h6
8.♗h4 g5 9.♘g5 hg5 10.♗g5 ♘bd7
11.g3 ♗b7 12.♗g2 ♕b6 13.ef6
0-0-0 14.0-0 ♗h6 15.♗e3 ♘f6
16.♕f3 ♗g7 17.a4 c5 18.dc5 ♗f3
19.cb6 ♗g2 20.♔g2 b4 21.ba7

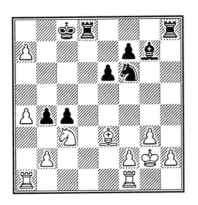

21...♔b7 22.♘b5 ♘g4 23.♖ac1
♖h2 24.♔f3 ♘e3 25.fe3 c3 26.bc3
bc3 27.♘c3 ♔a7 28.♘b5 ♔b6
29.♖c7 ♖f8 30.♖b1 ♗e5 31.a5 ♔a5
32.♘d6 ♔a6 33.♖c6 ♔a7 34.♖b7,
1-0

Game 193
Karpov, A—Timman, J
Brussels 1988

1.d4 d5 2.c4 dc4 3.e4 ♘f6 4.e5 ♘d5
5.♗c4 ♘b6 6.♗d3 ♘c6 7.♘e2 ♗g4
8.♗e3 ♗e2 9.♗e2 ♕d7 10.♘c3
0-0-0 11.a4 a6 12.a5 ♘d5 13.♗f3
♘db4 14.e6 ♕e6 15.d5 ♕e5 16.0-0
e6 17.dc6 ♖d1 18.cb7

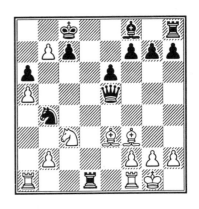

18...♔b8 19.♖fd1 ♗c5 20.♗c5 ♕c5
21.♖d7 f5 22.♖ad1 ♘c6 23.♘a4
♕b5 24.♖c1 ♕a4 25.♖c6 ♕a5
26.♖e6 ♔a7 27.g3 g5 28.♖h7 ♖b8
29.h3 g4 30.hg4 fg4 31.♗g2 ♕a1
32.♔h2 ♕b2 33.♖hh6 ♕a2
34.♖ef6 c5 35.♖f4 ♕d2 36.♗f1
♖b7 37.♖a6 ♔b8 38.♖f8 ♔c7
39.♗g2 ♕d7 40.♖h8 c4 41.♗e4,
1-0

Game 194
Timoshenko, Geo—Ruban, V
Tbilisi 1989

1.e4 c5 2.♘f3 d6 3.d4 cd4 4.♘d4
♘f6 5.♘c3 e6 6.♗e2 ♗e7 7.0-0 a6

8.f4 0-0 9.a4 ♘c6 10.♗e3 ♖e8
11.♔h1 ♕c7 12.♗f3 ♖b8 13.♕d2
♘a5 14.♕f2 ♘c4 15.♗c1 e5
16.♘de2 ♗d7 17.b3 ♘a5 18.f5 d5
19.♗g5 de4 20.♗f6 ef3 21.♘d5 fe2
22.♘c7 ef1=♕

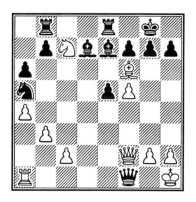

23.♖f1 ♗f6 24.♘d5 ♘c6 25.♘f6
gf6 26.♕h4 ♔g7 27.♖f3 ♖bd8
28.h3 ♘d4 29.♖g3 ♔f8 30.♕f6 ♘f5
31.♖g5 ♗e6 32.♕e5 ♖d5 33.♕h8
♔e7 34.♕h7 ♖ed8 35.♔h2 ♖e5
36.♖g8 ♖d2 37.♕h8 ♖ee2 38.♖e8
♔d6 39.♖d8 ♗d7 40.♕f6 ♔c5
41.♕c3 ♔d6 42.♕f6 ♔c5, 1/2-1/2

Game 195
Krausser,H—Gunter,D
corr. 1990

1.d4 d5 2.c4 c6 3.♘f3 e6 4.♘c3
♘f6 5.♗g5 dc4 6.e4 b5 7.e5 h6
8.♗h4 g5 9.♘g5 hg5 10.♗g5 ♘bd7
11.g3 ♗b7 12.♗g2 ♕b6 13.ef6
0-0-0 14.0-0 c5 15.d5 b4 16.♘a4
♕b5 17.a3 ♘b8 18.ab4 cb4
19.♕d4 ♘c6 20.dc6 ♖d4 21.cb7

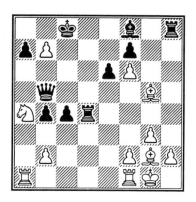

21...♔b8 22.♗e3 e5 23.b3 c3
24.♖ad1 ♗h6 25.♗d4 ed4 26.♖d4
c2 27.♖c4 c1=♕ 28.♖fc1 ♗c1
29.♖c1 ♖d8 30.♘c5 a5 31.h4 ♔a7
32.♘a4 ♖d5 33.♘b6, 1-0

Game 196
Thorhallsson,G—Gipslis
Gausdal 1992

1.e4 d6 2.d4 ♘f6 3.♘c3 g6 4.f4
♗g7 5.♘f3 0-0 6.♗e2 c5 7.0-0 cd4
8.♘d4 ♘bd7 9.♔h1 a6 10.♘f3 b6
11.e5 ♘e8 12.♗e3 ♗b7 13.e6 fe6
14.♘g5 ♘c7 15.♗c4 d5 16.♗b3
♘c5 17.♗d4 ♕d6 18.♗g7 ♔g7
19.♕d4 ♖f6 20.♘e2 ♖af8 21.♘f3
a5 22.♘e5 ♘b5 23.♕e3 a4 24.c4 d4
25.♕g1 d3 26.♖fd1 de2 27.♖d6
♘d6 28.♗d1 ed1=♕

(see next diagram)

29.♕d1 ♖f4 30.♔g1 ♖f2 31.♘f3
♖g2 32.♔g2 ♗f3 33.♕f3 ♖f3
34.♔f3 ♘c4 35.♖d1 ♘b2 36.♖d8,
0-1

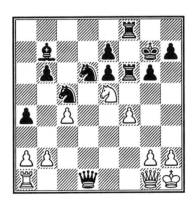

After 28...ed1=♕

Game 197
Pavlovic,M—Grivas,E
Karditsa 1994

1.c4 g6 2.g3 ♗g7 3.♗g2 e5 4.♘c3
d6 5.d3 ♘d7 6.e4 ♘e7 7.♘ge2 0-0
8.♗e3 f5 9.♕d2 ♘f6 10.♗g5 c6
11.0-0 ♗e6 12.♖ae1 ♕d7 13.b3 d5
14.f4 dc4 15.fe5 cd3 16.ef6 de2

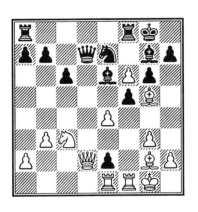

17.♕d7 ♗d7 18.♖e2 ♗f6 19.♗f6
♖f6 20.ef5 ♔f8 21.♖d2 ♗e8 22.g4
gf5 23.gf5 ♗f7 24.♖d7 ♖b8 25.♖e1
♘f5 26.♘e4 ♖g6 27.♖f1 ♖g2

28.♔g2 ♘e3 29.♔f2 ♘f1 30.♔f1
♗g6 31.♘c5 ♔e8 32.♖g7 ♖d8
33.♖b7 ♖d5 34.♘e6 ♖e5 35.♘d4
♗d3 36.♔f2 c5 37.♘c6 ♖e2
38.♔g3 ♖a2 39.♘a7 ♖b2 40.♘c8
c4 41.♘d6 ♔f8 42.bc4 ♖b7 43.♘b7
♗c4, 1/2-1/2

Game 198
Petursson—Thorhallsson,G
Iceland 1994

1.c4 c6 2.♘f3 d5 3.d4 ♘f6 4.♘c3
e6 5.♗g5 dc4 6.a4 b5 7.ab5 cb5
8.♘b5 ♕b6 9.♘c3 ♕b2 10.♗d2
♘d5 11.♘d5 ed5 12.♖b1 ♕a2
13.e4 ♗d6 14.♖b5 de4 15.♘e5
♗e6 16.d5 ♗e5 17.de6 ♘c6 18.ef7

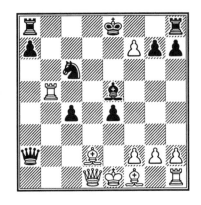

18...♔f8 19.♕c1 c3 20.♗c3 ♗c3
21.♕c3 ♘e7 22.♗c4 ♕a4 23.♖g5
♘g6 24.♖g6 hg6 25.♗d5 ♔e7
26.♕e5 ♔d7 27.0-0 ♖ad8, 1-0

Game 199
Kamsky, G—Kramnik, V
New York 1994

1.d4 d5 2.c4 c6 3.♘c3 ♘f6 4.♘f3
e6 5.♗g5 dc4 6.e4 b5 7.e5 h6
8.♗h4 g5 9.♘g5 hg5 10.♗g5 ♘bd7
11.ef6 ♗b7 12.g3 c5 13.d5 ♛b6
14.♗g2 0-0-0 15.0-0 b4 16.♘a4
♛b5 17.a3 ♘e5 18.ab4 cb4 19.♛d4
♘c6

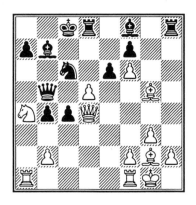

20.dc6 ♖d4 21.cb7 ♔c7 22.♗e3 e5
23.♘c3 bc3 24.bc3 ♗c5 25.cd4
♗d4 26.♖fb1 ♛c5 27.♖a6 ♖b8
28.♗c1 c3 29.♗a3 ♛c4 30.♗d6
♔d7 31.♗c6 ♔e6 32.♗b5 ♗f2
33.♔f2 ♛d4 34.♔f1 ♛e4 35.♖e1
♛h1 36.♔f2 ♛h2 37.♔f3 ♖b7
38.♗e5 ♖b6 39.♗c4 ♔d7 40.♖a7
♔c8 41.♖c7, 1-0

The e-pawn March

Game 200
Steinitz, W—Merian
New York 1884 (♖a1 odds)

1.e4 e5 2.♘c3 ♘c6 3.f4 ef4 4.d4
♛h4 5.♔e2 d5 6.ed5 ♗g4 7.♘f3
0-0-0 8.dc6 ♗c5 9.cb7

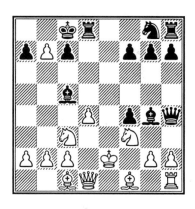

9...♔b7 10.♘b5 a6 11.b4 ♗b6
12.c3 ab5 13.♗f4 ♘f6 14.♗g3
♖he8 15.♔f2 ♘e4 16.♔g1 ♛f6
17.♗e1 ♗f3 18.gf3 ♛g5 19.♗g2
♛e3 20.♔f1 ♘c3 21.♛d2 ♗d4, 0-1

Game 201
Gunsberg, I—Schallopp, E
London 1886

1.e4 e5 2.♘f3 ♘c6 3.♗b5 ♘f6 4.d3
♘e7 5.c3 c6 6.♗a4 ♘g6 7.h4 h5
8.♗g5 ♛b6 9.♛e2 d5 10.ed5 ♗g4
11.dc6 0-0-0 12.cb7

(see next diagram)

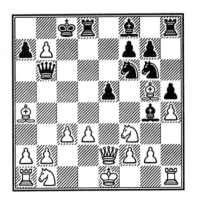

12...♔b8 13.0-0 ♕a6 14.♗c2 e4
15.♗f6 ef3 16.♗e5 ♘e5 17.♕e5
♗d6 18.♕e4 ♖he8 19.♕a4 fg2
20.♖c1 ♕b6 21.d4 ♗f4 22.♘a3
♗f3 23.♖e1 ♕f6, 0-1

Game 202
Charousek,R—Vollner
Kassa 1893

1.e4 e5 2.d4 ed4 3.c3 dc3 4.♗c4
♘f6 5.♘f3 ♗c5 6.♘c3 d6 7.0-0 0-0
8.♘g5 h6 9.♘f7 ♖f7 10.e5 ♘g4
11.e6 ♕h4 12.ef7

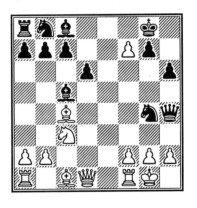

12...♔f8 13.♗f4 ♘f2 14.♕e2 ♘g4
15.♔h1 ♗d7 16.♖ae1 ♘c6 17.♕e8
♖e8 18.fe8=♕ ♗e8 19.♗d6#, 0-1

Game 203
Burn,A—Tarrasch,S
Hastings 1895

1.d4 d5 2.c4 e6 3.♘c3 c6 4.e3 f5
5.♘f3 ♗d6 6.c5 ♗c7 7.b4 ♘d7
8.♗b2 ♕e7 9.b5 ♕f6 10.a4 ♘e7
11.a5 a6 12.ba6 ba6 13.♕d2 e5
14.♘a4 e4 15.♘g1 f4 16.♘b6 fe3
17.fe3 0-0 18.0-0-0 ♖b8 19.♘e2
♘f5 20.♔c2 ♕h6 21.♗c1 ♘f6
22.g3 ♘g4 23.♖e1 ♘fe3 24.♔b1
♕g6 25.♘f4 ♗f4 26.gf4 ♘f1
27.♖ef1 e3 28.f5 ed2 29.fg6 ♗f5
30.♔a2 dc1=♕, 0-1

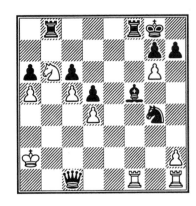

final position

Game 204
Tjunkov—Marakushkin
USSR 1962

1.c4 c5 2.♘c3 ♘f6 3.g3 d5 4.cd5
♘d5 5.♗g2 ♘c7 6.b3 ♘c6 7.♗b2

e5 8.♘f3 ♗e7 9.♘e4 f6 10.♖c1
b6 11.♘h4 ♕d7 12.g4 ♕g4 13.♘f6
gf6 14.♗c6 ♗d7 15.♗a8 ♘a8
16.♖c4 e4 17.♘f3 ♕g2 18.♖g1 ef3
(19.♖g2 fg2, △ 20...g1=♕#!), 0-1

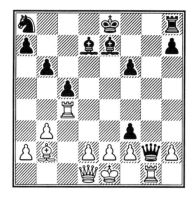

final position

Game 205
Popov,L—Bullovcic
Yugoslavia 1967

1.e4 ♘f6 2.e5 ♘d5 3.d4 d6 4.♘f3
♗g4 5.h3 ♗f3 6.♕f3 de5 7.de5 e6
8.♕e4 c6 9.♗c4 ♘d7 10.0-0 ♕c7
11.♖e1 h6 12.a4 a5 13.♘c3 ♘c3
14.bc3 ♖d8 15.f4 g6 16.g4 ♗c5
17.♔h1 ♘b6 18.f5 gf5 19.gf5 ef5
20.♕f5 ♘c4 21.e6 ♗d6 22.ef7

(see next diagram)

22...♔f8 23.♕f6 ♗e5 24.♗h6 ♖h6
25.♕h6 ♗g7 26.♖e8 ♖e8 27.♕g7
♔g7 28.fe8=♘, 1-0

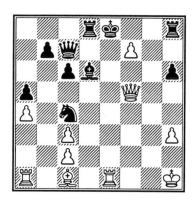

After 22.ef7

Game 206
Forintos—Bobocov
Hungary 1969

1.d4 ♘f6 2.c4 e6 3.♘c3 d5 4.♘f3
♗e7 5.♗f4 0-0 6.e3 b6 7.♗d3 ♗b7
8.0-0 c5 9.♕e2 ♘c6 10.dc5 bc5
11.♖fd1 ♕a5 12.a3 ♖fd8 13.h3
♖d7 14.♕c2 g6 15.cd5 ♘d5
16.♗b5 ♖ad8 17.♘e5 ♘c3 18.♖d7
♘b5 19.♘c6 ♗c6 20.♖e7 ♖d5
21.e4 ♘d4 22.ed5 ♘c2 23.dc6 ♔f8
24.♗d6 ♔g7 25.c7

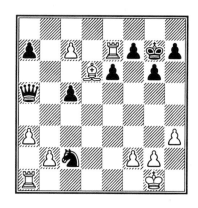

25...♕a6 26.♗e5 ♔h6 27.♖e8, 1-0

Game 207
Sosonko,G—Reihstein
Lugano 1976

1.d4 ♘f6 2.c4 g6 3.♘c3 d5 4.♘f3 ♗g7 5.♕b3 dc4 6.♕c4 0-0 7.e4 a6 8.♗e2 b5 9.♕b3 c5 10.dc5 ♗e6 11.♕c2 ♘c6 12.0-0 b4 13.♘a4 b3 14.ab3 ♘b4 15.♕d2 ♕a5 16.e5 ♖ad8 17.ef6 ♖d2 18.fg7 ♖e2 19.gf8=♕

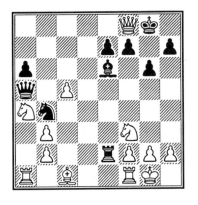

19...♔f8 20.♘c3 ♕c5 21.♗h6 ♔e8 22.♘e2 f6 23.♖ac1 ♕h5 24.♘f4 ♕h6 25.♘e6, 1-0

Game 208
Purins—Morgado,J
corr. 1976

1.e4 e5 2.♘f3 f5 3.♗c4 ♘f6 4.d4 fe4 5.♘e5 d5 6.♗e2 ♗e6 7.0-0 ♗d6 8.f3 ef3 9.♗f3 0-0 10.♕e2 ♕e7 11.♗g5 ♘bd7 12.♘c3 c6 13.♖ae1 ♖ae8 14.♗h5 ♗e5 15.de5

♕c5 16.♗e3 d4 17.♗e8 ♗c4 18.ef6 ♗e2 19.f7

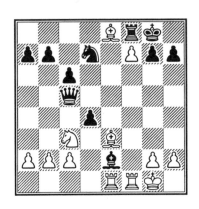

19...♔h8 20.♖e2 ♕c4 21.♖f4 c5 22.♗d4 cd4 23.♗d7 g5 24.♗e6 ♕c5 25.♖f5 ♕b6 26.♘a4 ♕d8 27.♗b3 b6 28.♖fe5 d3 29.cd3 ♕d4 30.♖2e3 h6 31.♖5e4, 1-0

Game 209
Pisarev—Sobol
Krasnoder 1978

1.e4 e5 2.♘f3 ♘c6 3.♗b5 a6 4.♗a4 ♘f6 5.0-0 b5 6.♗b3 ♘e4 7.d4 d5 8.de5 ♗e6 9.♘bd2 ♘c5 10.c3 d4 11.♗e6 ♘e6 12.♘e4 ♗e7 13.cd4 ♘cd4 14.♗e3 c5 15.b4 ♘f3 16.♕f3 c4 17.♖fd1 ♕c8 18.♘d6 ♗d6 19.ed6 0-0 20.d7

(see next diagram)

20...♕c7 21.a4 ba4 22.♗c5 ♘c5 23.bc5 ♖ab8 24.♕g3 ♕a5 25.c6 ♖b3 26.c7 ♖g3 27.d8=♕ ♖d3 28.♖d3 cd3 29.♕f8 ♔f8 30.c8=♕ ♔e7 31.♕c4 ♕e5 32.♖d1, 1-0

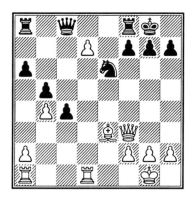

After 20.d7

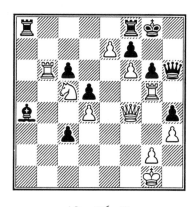

After 36.e7

Game 210
Marovic,D—Calvo
Osiek 1978

1.d4 d5 2.c4 dc4 3.♘f3 ♘f6 4.♘c3
a6 5.e4 b5 6.e5 ♘d5 7.a4 ♘c3
8.bc3 c6 9.♗e2 e6 10.♘g5 ♗e7
11.♘e4 ♘d7 12.♗a3 0-0 13.0-0
♘b6 14.♗e7 ♕e7 15.♘c5 ♘d5
16.♕d2 a5 17.♗f3 b4 18.♗d5 bc3
19.♕c3 ed5 20.♖ab1 ♗f5 21.♖b7
♕g5 22.f4 ♕g6 23.♖f3 ♖fb8
24.♕a5 h5 25.♕b6 ♖c8 26.♖g3
♕h7 27.♕b4 h4 28.♖g5 ♖e8
29.♖b6 ♗c2 30.h3 ♗b3 31.f5 ♕h6
32.♕d2 c3 33.♕f4 ♗a4 34.f6 g6
35.e6 ♖f8 36.e7

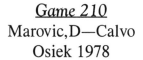

(see next diagram)

36...♖fe8 37.♘a4 ♖a4 38.♖c6 ♖c4
39.♖c4 dc4 40.d5 c2 41.d6 ♖b8
42.d7 ♖b1 43.♔h2, 1-0

Game 211
Wolf,S—Gebric
corr. 1988

1.e4 e6 2.d4 d5 3.e5 c5 4.c3 ♕b6
5.♘f3 ♗d7 6.♗e2 ♗b5 7.c4 ♗c4
8.♗c4 ♕b4 9.♘bd2 dc4 10.a3 ♕a5
11.0-0 ♘c6 12.♘c4 ♕a6 13.♘d6
♗d6 14.ed6 cd4 15.d7

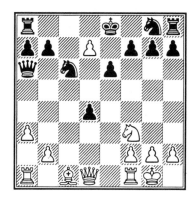

15...♔e7 16.♘d4 ♘f6 17.♘f5 ef5
18.♖e1 ♔d8 19.♗f4 ♘e7 20.♖c1
♘fd5 21.♖e7 ♘f4 22.♕e1 ♕d6
23.♖f7 ♕e6 24.♕a5 b6 25.♕a7

♕e1 26.♖e1 ♖a7 27.♖e8 ♖e8
28.de8=♕ ♔e8 29.♖a7, 1-0

Game 212
Polgar,S—Palatnik,S
Rome 1989

1.e4 ♘f6 2.e5 ♘d5 3.d4 d6 4.♘f3
♗g4 5.♗e2 e6 6.0-0 ♗e7 7.c4 ♘b6
8.♘c3 0-0 9.♗e3 d5 10.c5 ♗f3
11.gf3 ♘c8 12.f4 ♘c6 13.♖b1 ♗h4
14.♔h1 ♘8e7 15.♗d3 g6 16.♕g4
♘f5 17.♗f5 ef5 18.♕f3 ♘e7
19.♕h3 ♘c8 20.♖g1 ♔h8 21.b4 a6
22.a4 c6 23.b5 ab5 24.ab5 ♖a3
25.♖gc1 ♗e7 26.b6 ♗c5 27.dc5 d4
28.♖d1 ♖c3 29.♕h6 ♖c5 30.♗d4
♖d5 31.♔g2 ♘e7 32.♗c5 ♖e8
33.♖dc1 ♖d3 34.♗d6 ♘c8 35.♖d1
♖d1 36.♖d1 ♖g8 37.♖d3 ♘b6
38.e6 f6 39.e7

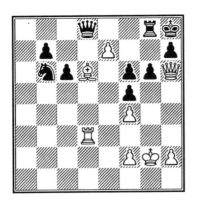

39...♕e8 40.♕f8 ♘d5 41.♖d5 ♖f8
42.ef8=♕ ♕f8 43.♗f8 cd5 44.♔f3
♔g8 45.♗b4 g5 46.♔e3 ♔f7
47.♔d4 ♔g6 48.♗e7 h6 49.♔d5
♔h5 50.♗f6 ♔g4 51.fg5 hg5
52.♔e5 b5 53.♗e7, 1-0

Game 213
Ivanchuk,V—Kramnik,V
Linares 1998

1.e4 c5 2.♘f3 ♘c6 3.d4 cd4 4.♘d4
♘f6 5.♘c3 d6 6.♗c4 ♕b6 7.♘db5
a6 8.♗e3 ♕d8 9.♘d4 ♘g4 10.♘c6
bc6 11.♕f3 ♘e5 12.♕e2 e6
13.0-0-0 ♗e7 14.♗d4 ♕c7 15.♗e5
de5 16.♘a4 0-0 17.♖d3 ♕a5 18.b3
♖b8 19.♕d2 ♕d2 20.♔d2 g6
21.♖d1 ♔g7 22.♔e2 a5 23.♖c3
♗b4 24.♖cd3 ♗e7 25.g3 h5 26.h4
f5 27.♖c3 ♗b4 28.♖e3 ♔f6 29.f4
ef4 30.gf4 ♗e7 31.e5 ♔f7 32.♖ed3
♗h4 33.♘c5 ♗e7 34.♖d6 ♗d6
35.ed6 ♖d8 36.d7 ♔e7 37.dc8=♘

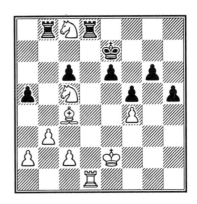

37...♖bc8 38.♖d8 ♖d8 39.♘e6
♖h8 40.♘g5 h4 41.♘h3 ♔f6
42.♔f2 ♖d8 43.♗d3 a4 44.♘g5 a3
45.♘f3 c5 46.♘g5 ♖d4 47.♔f3 ♖d7
48.♔e3 ♖d8 49.♘f3 ♖e8 50.♔f2
♖d8 51.♘h4 c4 52.bc4 ♖b8 53.c5
♖b2 54.c6 ♔e7 55.♘g6 ♔d6
56.♘e5 ♖a2 57.♘c4 ♔c7 58.♔g3
♖a1 59.♘a3 ♖a3 60.♔h4 ♔c6

61.♔g5 ♖a5 62.♗f5 ♔d6 63.♔g4
♔e7 = (...), 1/2-1/2

The f-pawn March

Game 214
Morphy,P—De Riviere,J
Paris 1863

1.e4 e5 2.♘f3 ♘c6 3.♗c4 ♘f6 4.d4
ed4 5.0-0 ♗e7 6.♘d4 0-0 7.♘c3
♘e5 8.♗e2 d5 9.f4 ♘c6 10.♘c6
bc6 11.e5 ♗c5 12.♔h1 ♘d7
13.♗d3 ♖e8 14.♗d2 ♘f8 15.♕h5
g6 16.♕h6 ♘e6 17.f5 ♗f8 18.♕h3
♘c5 19.e6 fe6 20.f6 e5 21.f7 ♔h8
22.fe8=♕

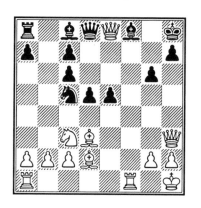

22...♕e8 23.♗g6 ♗h3 24.♗e8 ♗g2
25.♔g2 ♖e8 26.♖ae1, 1-0

Game 215
Zukertort,J—Blackburne,J
London 1883

1.c4 e6 2.e3 ♘f6 3.♘f3 b6 4.♗e2
♗b7 5.0-0 d5 6.d4 ♗d6 7.♘c3 0-0

8.b3 ♘bd7 9.♗b2 ♕e7 10.♘b5
♘e4 11.♘d6 cd6 12.♘d2 ♘df6
13.f3 ♘d2 14.♕d2 dc4 15.♗c4 d5
16.♗d3 ♖fc8 17.♖ae1 ♖c7 18.e4
♖ac8 19.e5 ♘e8 20.f4 g6 21.♖e3 f6
22.ef6 ♘f6 23.f5 ♘e4 24.♗e4 de4
25.fg6 ♖c2 26.gh7

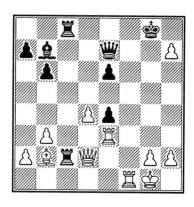

26...♔h8 27.d5 e5 28.♕b4 ♖8c5
29.♖f8 ♔h7 30.♕e4 ♔g7 31.♗e5
♔f8 32.♗g7, 1-0

Game 216
Charousek,R—Schaffer
Kassa 1892

1.e4 e5 2.♘f3 d6 3.d4 ♗g4 4.de5
♗f3 5.♕f3 de5 6.♗c4 ♕f6 7.♕b3
b6 8.♘c3 ♗c5 9.0-0 ♘e7 10.♗e3
♗d6 11.♘b5 0-0 12.♘d6 cd6 13.f4
♕g6 14.f5 ♕g4 15.f6 ♘ec6 16.♗d5
♕d7 17.♗h6 ♘d4 18.fg7 ♘bc6
19.gf8=♕

(see next diagram)

19...♖f8 20.♕g3, 1-0

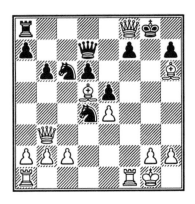

After 19.gf8=♕

Game 217
Blackburne—Walbrodt,C
Hastings 1895

1.e4 e5 2.♗e2 ♘c6 3.♘f3 ♘f6
4.d3 d5 5.ed5 ♘d5 6.0-0 ♗e7
7.♘c3 0-0 8.♘e1 f5 9.♘d5 ♕d5
10.♗f3 ♕e6 11.♗c6 ♕c6 12.♘f3
♗f6 13.♗g5 e4 14.♗f6 ♖f6 15.♘e5
♕b5 16.♘c4 ♗e6 17.b3 ♖d8
18.♕e2 ed3 19.cd3 f4 20.♘e5 f3
21.♕e3 fg2

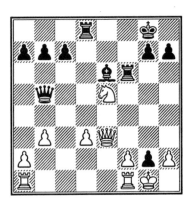

22.♔g2 ♖h6 23.♔h1 ♖h5 24.♖ae1
♗h3 25.♖g1 ♕d5 26.♘f3 ♖f8
27.♖g3 ♗d7 28.♕e7 g6 29.♕e4
♗c6 30.♔g1 ♕f7 31.♕b4 ♗f3
32.♖e7 ♕f6 33.♕e1 ♗d5 34.♖c7
♖h2 35.f3 ♕h4, 0-1

Game 218
Spielmann,R—Gruenfeld,E
Baden-Baden 1914

1.e4 e5 2.♘f3 ♘c6 3.♗c4 ♗c5
4.d4 ♗d4 5.♘d4 ♘d4 6.0-0 ♘f6
7.f4 d6 8.fe5 de5 9.♗g5 ♕e7
10.♘c3 c6 11.♕d3 ♗e6 12.♗e6
♘e6 13.♗f6 gf6 14.♘e2 ♖g8 15.c3
♖d8 16.♕f3 ♖d2 17.b4 ♕d8 18.♖f2
♖g6 19.♘g3 ♕b6 20.♔f1 ♕b5
21.♔g1 ♖d3 22.♕f5 ♘f4 23.a4
♕b6 24.a5 ♕d8 25.♖af1 ♖c3
26.♔h1 ♖g5 27.♕h7 ♖cg3 28.♖f4
ef4 29.hg3 ♕d3 30.♕h8 ♔e7
31.♔g1 ♕d4 32.♔h2 ♕e5 33.g4
♖g4 34.♖d1 f3 35.♔h1 fg2

36.♔g1 ♕c7 37.♕h5 ♖g5 38.♕h3
c5 39.♖d5 cb4 40.♖g5 fg5 41.♕f5
♕g3 42.♕c5 ♔f6 43.♕f8 b3 44.e5

♕e5 45.♕h8 ♔f5 46.♕h3 ♔g6
47.♕b3 ♕e2, 0-1

Game 219
Nimzowitsch,A—Rubinstein,A
Berlin 1928

1.♘f3 d5 2.b3 ♗f5 3.♗b2 e6 4.g3
h6 5.♗g2 ♘d7 6.0-0 ♘gf6 7.d3
♗e7 8.e3 0-0 9.♕e2 c6 10.♔h1 a5
11.a4 ♘c5 12.♘d4 ♗h7 13.f4 ♘fd7
14.♘d2 ♕c7 15.e4 de4 16.♘e4
♘e4 17.de4 e5 18.♘f3 ef4 19.gf4
♖fe8 20.e5 ♘c5 21.♘d4 ♘e6
22.♖ad1 ♘d4 23.♗d4 ♗f5 24.♗e4
♗e4 25.♕e4 ♖ad8 26.e6 ♗f8
27.♗e5 ♕c8 28.f5 fe6 29.f6 ♖d1
30.f7

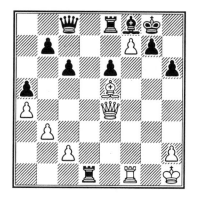

30...♔h8 31.♖d1 ♖d8 32.♕g6, 1-0

Game 220
Bogoljubow,E—Kashdan,I
Stockholm 1930

1.d4 e6 2.c4 ♘f6 3.♘c3 d5 4.♘f3
♘bd7 5.♗f4 dc4 6.e3 ♘d5 7.♗c4
♘f4 8.ef4 ♘b6 9.0-0 ♗e7 10.♗b3
0-0 11.♖e1 c5 12.dc5 ♘d7 13.c6

bc6 14.♘d4 ♘b8 15.♘a4 ♕d6
16.g3 ♖d8 17.♘f3 ♗b7 18.f5 c5
19.fe6 c4 20.ef7

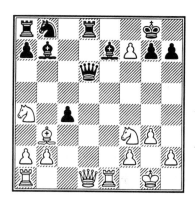

20...♔f8 21.♗c2 ♕f6! ∓ 22.♘d2
♖d2 23.♕d2 ♕f3 24.♗e4 ♗e4
25.♖e4 ♕e4 26.♘c3 ♕f5 27.♕e2
♘c6 28.♖d1 ♖d8 29.♖d8 ♘d8
30.♕c4 ♘f7 31.f4 g5 32.fg5 ♗c5
33.♔g2 ♕f2 34.♔h3 ♘g5 35.♔g4
♕f3 36.♔h4 ♕f5 37.g4 ♗f2, 0-1

Game 221
Konstantinopolsky,A—Chistiakov,A
corr. 1935

1.e4 c5 2.♘f3 ♘c6 3.d4 cd4 4.♘d4
♘f6 5.♘c3 d6 6.♗g5 e6 7.♕d2
♗e7 8.0-0-0 0-0 9.f4 a6 10.♗f6 ♗f6
11.♘c6 bc6 12.♕d6 ♕b6 13.♘a4
♕e3 14.♔b1 ♗b7 15.♗d3 ♖fd8
16.♕c7 ♖ab8 17.♘b6 ♗a8 18.♘c4
♕c5 19.e5 ♗e7 20.♘d6 ♗d6
21.ed6 a5 22.d7 g6 23.♖he1 ♕b4
24.b3 c5 25.♗c4 ♗g2 26.f5 ♗f3
27.fe6 ♗d1 28.ef7 ♔g7 29.f8=♕

(see next diagram)

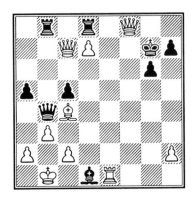

29...♖f8 30.d8=♕ ♔h6 31.♕d1
♕c4 32.♕d2, 1-0

Game 222
Tringov,G—Planinc
Yugoslavia 1999

1.e4 e6 2.d4 d5 3.♘c3 ♗b4 4.e5
♕d7 5.a3 ♗c3 6.bc3 b6 7.a4 ♗a6
8.♗a6 ♘a6 9.♕g4 f5 10.♕h5 g6
11.♕e2 ♘b8 12.h4 h6 13.♘f3 ♘c6
14.c4 dc4 15.♕c4 ♘ge7 16.♗b2
♘d5 17.♘d2 ♘a5 18.♕b5 c6
19.♕e2 0-0-0 20.♘c4 ♘c4 21.♕c4
♘c7 22.0-0 g5 23.h5 g4 24.♕b3 f4
25.c4 ♕e7 26.a5 ♕h4 27.ab6 g3
28.♖fd1 ♕h2 29.♔f1 f3 30.♔e1 fg2
31.♔d2 g1=♕

(see next diagram)

32.♖g1 ♕f2 33.♔c3 ♕d4 34.♔b4
♘d5 35.♔a4 ♘b6 36.♔b4 a5
37.♔a3 ♘c4 38.♔a2 ♘b2 39.♖ac1
♕a4 40.♕a4 ♘a4 41.♖c6 ♔d7
42.♖a6 ♖a8, 0-1

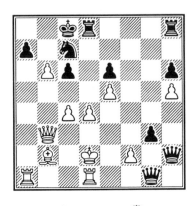

After 31...g1=♕

Game 223
Ljubojevic,L—Milicevic
Yugoslavia 1974

1.e4 c5 2.♘f3 d6 3.d4 cd4 4.♘d4
♘f6 5.♘c3 a6 6.♗g5 e6 7.f4 ♕c7
8.♗f6 gf6 9.♗e2 b5 10.♗h5 b4
11.♘ce2 ♗g7 12.f5 0-0 13.fe6 fe6
14.♘f4 ♕e7 15.0-0 e5 16.♘f5 ♕a7
17.♔h1 ♗f5 18.ef5 ef4 19.♗f3 ♘d7
20.♗a8 ♕a8 21.♕d6 ♘e5 22.♖f4
a5 23.♖d1 ♘f7 24.♕d5 ♕a7
25.♕e6 ♕b8 26.♖g4 ♔h8 27.♖gd4
♘e5 28.h3 ♕c7 29.♖1d2 ♗h6
30.♖d8 ♕f7 31.♖2d7 ♕e6 32.fe6
♘d7 33.e7

(see next diagram)

33...♔g7 34.♖f8, 1-0

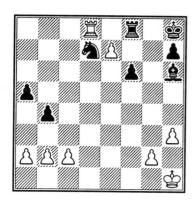

After 33.e7

Game 224
Dolmatov,S—Ristic
Tallin 1977

1.e4 c5 2.♘f3 d6 3.d4 ♘f6 4.♘c3
cd4 5.♘d4 g6 6.♗e2 ♗g7 7.0-0
♘c6 8.♘b3 0-0 9.♗g5 ♗e6 10.f4
♘a5 11.f5 ♗c4 12.♔h1 ♖c8 13.e5
♗e2 14.♘e2 ♘e4 15.♘a5 ♘g5
16.f6 ♕a5 17.fe7

17...♖fe8 18.ed6 ♖b8 19.♕d3 ♗e5
20.♖ad1 ♘e6 21.♕f3 ♘g5 22.♕e3
f6 23.b4 ♕b4 24.d7 ♖e7 25.d8=♕

♖d8 26.♕b3 ♕b3 27.♖d8 ♔f7
28.ab3 ♗c7 29.♖c8 ♗h2 30.♔h2
♖e2 31.♖f4 ♖e7 32.♖b4 ♘e4 33.c4
f5 34.c5 ♔f6 35.♖c4 ♔g5 36.b4 f4
37.b5 ♔g4 38.♖f8 g5 39.c6 bc6
40.bc6 ♘d6 41.c7, 1-0

Game 225
Pavlov—Kharitonov,A
corr. 1984

1.e4 c5 2.♘f3 ♘c6 3.d4 cd4 4.♘d4
♘f6 5.♘c3 d6 6.♗c4 e6 7.♗e3 ♗e7
8.♕e2 0-0 9.0-0-0 ♕c7 10.♗b3 a6
11.g4 ♘d4 12.♖d4 ♘d7 13.g5 b5
14.♕h5 ♖d8 15.♖g1 ♘c5 16.e5 g6
17.♕h3 d5 18.♖h4 ♕e5 19.♗d4
♘b3 20.ab3 ♕f5 21.♕g3 ♗b7
22.♔b1 ♗d6 23.f4 h5 24.gh6 ♔h7
25.♘d1 ♖ac8 26.♘e3 ♕e4 27.♕g5
♕d4 28.f5 ♕e5 29.fg6 ♔h8 30.g7
♔h7 31.g8=♕

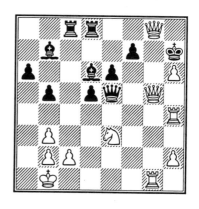

31...♖g8 32.♕g7 ♖g7 33.hg7 ♔g8
34.♖h8#, 1-0

Game 226
Chandler,M—Vaganian,R
London 1986

1.e4 e6 2.d4 d5 3.♘c3 ♗b4 4.e5
c5 5.a3 ♗a5 6.b4 cd4 7.♘b5 ♗c7
8.f4 ♗d7 9.♘f3 ♗b5 10.♗b5 ♘c6
11.0-0 ♘ge7 12.♗d3 a6 13.♔h1 h6
14.♕e2 ♕d7 15.♗b2 ♗b6 16.♖ae1
♖c8 17.g4 g6 18.♘h4 h5 19.f5 hg4
20.fg6 ♖h4 21.gf7

21...♔f8 22.♗c1 ♘f5 23.♗f5 d3
24.♗d3 g3 25.♕g2 ♖h2 26.♕h2
gh2 27.♗h6 ♔e7 28.♗g5 ♔f8
29.♗h6 ♔e7 30.♗g6 ♗c7 31.♗g5
♔f8 32.♗h6 ♔e7 33.f8=♕ ♖f8
34.♗f8 ♔d8 35.♖f7 ♕e8 36.♗g7
♘e5 37.♗f6, 1-0

Game 227
Panov,V—Yudovich,M
Tbilisi 1937

1.e4 e6 2.d4 d5 3.♘c3 ♘f6 4.♗g5
♗e7 5.e5 ♘fd7 6.h4 f6 7.♗d3 c5
8.♕h5 ♔f8 9.♘d5 fg5 10.♖h3 g4

11.♘f4 ♘e5 12.de5 gh3 13.♗h7
♖h7 14.♕h7 h2 15.♔e2 h1=♕

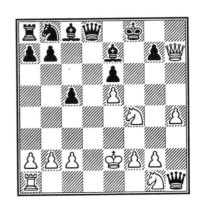

16.♘g6 ♔f7 17.♘h8 ♕h8 18.♕h8
♘c6 19.♕h5 ♔g8 20.♘h3 ♕g2
21.♕e8 ♗f8 22.♘g5 ♘e5 23.c4
♕g4 24.♔f1 ♕c4 25.♔g1 ♕g4
26.♔f1 ♗d7, 0-1

The g-pawn March

Game 228
Ragozin,V—Levenfish,G
Leningrad 1932

1.d4 ♘f6 2.c4 e6 3.♘c3 ♗b4 4.♕c2
d5 5.cd5 ed5 6.♗g5 ♗e6 7.e3
♘bd7 8.f4 h6 9.♗h4 g5 10.f5 ♗f5
11.♕f5 gh4 12.♗d3 ♕e7 13.♘f3 h3
14.0-0 hg2

(see next diagram)

15.♖f2 ♗c3 16.bc3 ♖g8 17.♖b1
0-0-0 18.♘e5 ♕e6 19.♕f4 ♘e4
20.♗e4 de4 21.♕e4 ♘b6 22.♕f3 f6

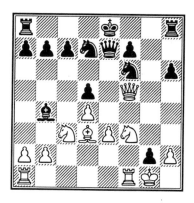

After 14...hg2

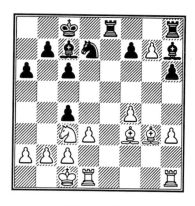

After 23.fg7

23.♘d3 ♕g4 24.♕g4 ♖g4 25.♘c5
♖e8 26.♖f6 ♘d5 27.♖f2 b6 28.♘d3
♖e3 29.♘e5 ♖g8 30.♖g2 ♖g2
31.♔g2 ♖e2 32.♔g3 ♘c3 33.♖f1
♖a2 34.♖f8 ♔b7, 0-1

Game 229
Rabinovitch,I—Kachn,I
Moscow 1935

1.e4 e5 2.♘f3 ♘f6 3.♘e5 d6 4.♘f3
♘e4 5.♕e2 ♕e7 6.d3 ♘f6 7.♗g5
♕e2 8.♗e2 ♗e7 9.♘c3 ♗g4
10.0-0-0 ♘bd7 11.h3 ♗h5 12.g4
♗g6 13.♘d4 0-0-0 14.f4 h6 15.♗h4
♖de8 16.♗f3 ♗d8 17.♗g3 a6
18.♘b3 ♗h7 19.♘a5 c6 20.♘c4
♗c7 21.g5 d5 22.gf6 dc4 23.fg7

(see next diagram)

23...♖hg8 24.dc4 ♖g7 25.♗h2 ♗f5
26.♖he1 ♘f6 27.♖e8 ♘e8 28.h4
♗g4 29.♖e1 ♗f3 30.♖e8 ♔d7
31.♖e3 ♖g2 32.♖f3 ♖h2 33.♘e4
♖h4, 0-1

Game 230
Kotov,A—Tolush,A
Leningrad 1956

1.d4 ♘f6 2.c4 e6 3.♘f3 c5 4.d5 ed5
5.cd5 d6 6.♘c3 ♗e7 7.♘d2 0-0
8.♘c4 ♘e8 9.♗f4 ♗f6 10.e3 ♘d7
11.♗e2 ♘b6 12.0-0 ♘c4 13.♗c4
♘c7 14.♕e2 a6 15.a4 b6 16.♘e4
♗e7 17.♕h5 g6 18.♕f3 f5 19.♘c3
♖b8 20.♗h6 ♖f7 21.♕e2 ♗f6
22.♖fd1 ♗b7 23.♗f4 ♕d7 24.♗g3
♖e8 25.♕c2 g5 26.♘e2 ♗c8 27.h4
h6 28.♗h2 ♖e4 29.h5 ♖e8 30.♗d3
♖ef8 31.♕b3 b5 32.♗c2 b4
33.♗d3 ♘e8 34.♘g3 ♗e5 35.♘f1
♗h2 36.♔h2 ♘f6 37.♗e2 ♖e7
38.♘d2 f4 39.♘c4 g4 40.♕d3 f3
41.♗f1 g3 42.♔g1 gf2

(see next diagram)

43.♔h1 ♘e4, 0-1

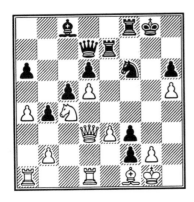

After 42...gf2

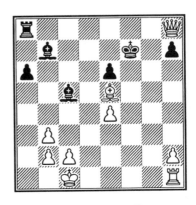

After 27.gh8=♕

Game 231
Medina—Pomar,A
Malaga 1969

1.e4 c5 2.♘f3 d6 3.d4 ♘f6 4.♘c3
cd4 5.♘d4 ♘c6 6.♗c4 ♕c7 7.♗b3
a6 8.♗e3 e6 9.♕e2 ♗e7 10.0-0-0
♘a5 11.g4 ♘b3 12.ab3 b5 13.g5
♘d7 14.♘f5 b4 15.♘g7 ♔f8
16.♕h5 ♔g7 17.♗d4 ♘e5 18.f4
bc3 19.♗c3 ♗b7 20.fe5 de5
21.♖d7 ♕d7 22.♕h6 ♔g8 23.♗e5
f6 24.gf6 ♗c5 25.♕g7 ♕g7 26.fg7
♔f7 27.gh8=♕

(see next diagram)

27...♖h8 28.♗h8 ♗e4 29.♖f1 ♗f5
30.♗e5 ♗e3 31.♔b1 ♔g6 32.♗f4
♗d4 33.♖e1 ♔h5 34.♔c1 ♔g4
35.♗e5 ♗f2 36.♖f1 ♗e3 37.♔d1
♗c5 38.♖f4 ♔h3 39.♖f3 ♔g2
40.♖g3 ♔f2 41.♔d2 h5 42.♖g8 a5
43.c4 h4 44.♖c8 ♗e3 45.♔c3 ♔e2
46.b4 ♗d2 47.♔b3 ♗b4 48.c5 ♗e4

49.c6 ♔e3 50.♔a4 ♗d5 51.♔b5
♔e4 52.♗f6 h3 53.♖d8 ♔e3
54.♖d5, 1-0

Game 232
Schteinbok—Koppe
corr. 1973

1.h4 d5 2.c3 c5 3.e3 ♘c6 4.d3 ♘f6
5.♗e2 e6 6.♘d2 ♗d6 7.a3 ♕c7
8.b4 b6 9.♗b2 ♗b7 10.♘gf3 e5
11.e4 0-0 12.♘g5 h6 13.♘h3 ♖ad8
14.g4 cb4 15.g5 bc3 16.♗c3 ♘e4
17.de4 de4 18.gh6 e3 19.hg7

19...ef2 20.♔f2 ♖fe8 21.♗c4, 1-0

Game 233
Pestic—Bernstein,S
Philadelphia 1978

1.♘f3 b6 2.g3 ♗b7 3.♗g2 c5 4.d3 g6 5.0-0 ♗g7 6.e4 ♘c6 7.♘bd2 ♘h6 8.♘h4 0-0 9.f4 f5 10.e5 ♕c7 11.♘df3 ♖ad8 12.c3 ♘f7 13.♖e1 e6 14.d4 cd4 15.cd4 ♘b4 16.♖e2 ♗a6 17.♖d2 ♖c8 18.a3 ♘c2 19.♖b1 ♘e3 20.♕b3 ♕c1 21.♖c1 ♖c1 22.♘e1 ♖e1 23.♔f2 ♘g2 24.♘g2 ♖f1 25.♔e3 ♘h6 26.h3 g5 27.♖d1 g4 28.♖f1 ♗f1 29.♔f2 gh3 30.♘e1 h2

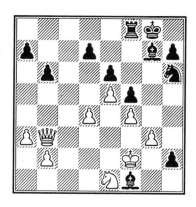

31.♕f3 ♗c4 32.♕g2 ♘g4, 0-1

Game 234
Atalik,S—Miles,A
Heraklio 1993

1.d4 ♘f6 2.c4 g6 3.♘c3 ♗g7 4.e4 d6 5.f3 0-0 6.♗e3 c5 7.♘ge2 ♘c6 8.♕d2 e6 9.♖d1 b6 10.♗g5 ♗a6 11.d5 ♘e5 12.b3 h6 13.♗e3 ed5

14.♘d5 ♘d5 15.♕d5 b5 16.cb5 ♗b5 17.♘c1 ♗c6 18.♕d2 f5 19.♕d6 ♕e8 20.♕c5 fe4 21.f4 ♘d3 22.♘d3 ed3 23.♔f2 ♖c8 24.♕c4 ♔h8 25.♕d3 g5 26.♖c1 ♖d8 27.♕e2 gf4 28.♗c5 f3 29.♕e8 fg2 30.♗f8 gh1=♘, 0-1

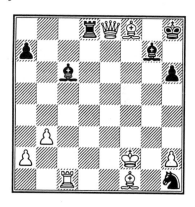

final position

The h-pawn March

Game 235
Morphy,P—Perrin
New York 1860 (♘b1 odds)

1.e4 e5 2.♘f3 ♘c6 3.♗c4 ♘f6 4.d4 ed4 5.0-0 ♘e4 6.♗d5 ♘f6 7.♘g5 ♘d5 8.♖e1 ♗e7 9.♕h5 ♖f8 10.♘h7 ♘f6 11.♘f6 gf6 12.♕h7 ♘e5 13.♗h6 ♘g6 14.h4 d5 15.h5 ♖h8 16.hg6 ♖h7 17.gh7 ♔d7 18.♗g7 ♔d6 19.h8=♕

(see next diagram)

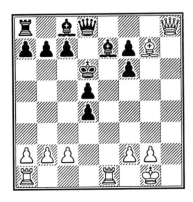

19...♕h8 20.♗h8 ♗f5 21.♗g7 ♖g8
22.♗h6 ♗c2 23.♗f4 ♔d7 24.♗c7
♗e4 25.♗g3 ♗d6 26.♗d6 ♔d6
27.f3 ♗f3 28.♔f2 ♗e4 29.♖g1 d3
30.♔e3 ♔e5 31.♖ac1 f5 32.♖c7 f4
33.♔d2 f3 34.g4 f5 35.g5 ♔f4
36.g6 ♖g6 37.♖g6 f2 38.♖c1 ♔f3
39.♖h1 ♔f4 40.♖f1 ♔f3 41.♖g7 d4
42.a4 a6 43.b4 b5 44.a5 ♗d5
45.♖g6 ♔f4 46.♖c1 ♗e4 47.♖a6
♗g2 48.♔d3 f1=♕ 49.♖f1 ♗f1
50.♔d4 ♗c4 51.♖f6 ♔g5 52.♔e5
♗d3 53.a6 ♗e4 54.a7 ♔g4 55.♖f5,
1-0

Game 236
Karstanien—Anderssen,A
Cologne 1860

1.e4 e5 2.♘f3 ♘c6 3.♗c4 ♗c5 4.b4
♗b4 5.c3 ♗c5 6.d4 ed4 7.0-0 d6
8.cd4 ♗b6 9.d5 ♘a5 10.e5 ♘e7
11.♘c3 ♘c4 12.♕a4 ♗d7 13.♕c4
0-0 14.♘e4 ♗f5 15.♗b2 ♗e4
16.♕e4 ♘g6 17.♖ad1 ♕e7 18.g3
♖ae8 19.♕d3 de5 20.♗a3 ♗c5
21.♗c5 ♕c5 22.♖fe1 h6 23.♕f5

♕d6 24.♖d3 ♖e7 25.♘d2 ♕a6
26.♘e4 ♕a2 27.h4 ♕a6 28.h5
♖ee8 29.d6 ♔h8 30.♖ed1 cd6
31.hg6 d5 32.gf7

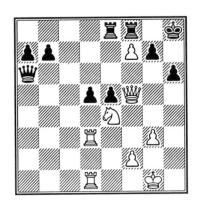

32...♖e7 33.♖d5 ♖ef7 34.♕e5 ♕e2
35.♖5d2 ♕f3 36.♖d7 ♔h7 37.♖1d3
♕g4 38.♖f7 ♖f7 39.♘c3 ♖d7
40.♖d7 ♕d7 41.♕e4 ♔h8 42.♕a4
♕c8, 1/2-1/2

Game 237
Lasker,Em—Blackburne,J
Hastings 1895

1.e4 e5 2.♘f3 ♘c6 3.♗b5 d6 4.d4
♗d7 5.♘c3 ed4 6.♘d4 ♘d4 7.♕d4
♗b5 8.♘b5 ♘e7 9.0-0 ♘c6 10.♕c3
a6 11.♘a3 ♕f6 12.♕b3 0-0-0 13.c4
♖e8 14.♖e1 ♕g6 15.♗d2 ♗e7
16.♕c2 ♗f6 17.♖ab1 ♗d4 18.b4
♘e5 19.♖e2 ♘f3 20.♔h1 ♘h2
21.♗f4 ♘g4 22.♗g3 ♗e5 23.♕d3
♗g3 24.♕g3 ♘f6 25.♕h3 ♔b8
26.f3 ♘h5 27.♖d2 ♖e5 28.♔g1 ♘f4
29.♕h4 ♘e6 30.♖d5 ♘g5 31.♕g3
♖d5 32.cd5 h5 33.b5 h4 34.♕g4
ab5 35.♘b5 h3 36.♖b2 hg2

37.♖g2 ♘h3 38.♔f1 ♕f6 39.e5 de5
40.♖h2 e4 41.♖h3 ♕a1 42.♔g2 ef3
43.♔g3 ♕e5 44.♔f3 ♕d5, 0-1

Game 238
Chigorin,M—Pillsbury,H
St. Petersburg 1895

1.e4 e5 2.♘f3 ♘c6 3.♗b5 g6 4.♘c3
♗g7 5.d3 ♘ge7 6.♗g5 f6 7.♗e3 a6
8.♗a4 b5 9.♗b3 ♘a5 10.♕d2 ♘b3
11.ab3 ♗b7 12.♗h6 0-0 13.h4 d6
14.0-0-0 c5 15.g4 b4 16.♘b1 a5
17.♖dg1 a4 18.ba4 ♖a4 19.♕e3
♘c6 20.♗g7 ♔g7 21.g5 ♘d4 22.h5
♘f3 23.hg6 ♘g1 24.gf6 ♔f6 25.gh7

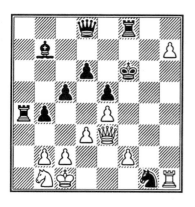

25...♔e6 26.♖g1 ♔d7 27.♕h3 ♔c6
28.♕e6 ♖a8 29.♖g7 ♔b6 30.♘a3
♗a6 31.♖d7 ♕d7 32.♕d7 ♖ad8
33.♕g7 ba3 34.ba3 c4 35.d4 ♖f2
36.h8=♕ ♖h8 37.♕h8 ♖f1 38.♔b2
ed4 39.♕d4 ♔c7 40.a4 ♖f7 41.a5
♔c8 42.♕d6 ♖b7 43.♔c3 ♗b5
44.a6 ♖c7 45.a7, 1-0

Game 239
Panov,V—Solutren
Moscow 1952

1.e4 e5 2.♘f3 ♘c6 3.♗b5 a6 4.♗a4
d6 5.c3 ♗d7 6.d4 ♗e7 7.0-0 ♗f6
8.♗c2 h6 9.♗e3 ♘ge7 10.♘bd2
0-0 11.d5 ♘b8 12.♘e1 g5 13.c4
♘g6 14.c5 ♘f4 15.♘c4 ♗b5 16.b3
♘d7 17.cd6 cd6 18.g3 ♘g6 19.♖c1
♕e7 20.♘g2 ♗g7 21.♗d2 ♗c4
22.bc4 ♖fc8 23.♘e3 ♗f8 24.♗b3
♘f6 25.♕f3 ♘e8 26.♘f5 ♕f6
27.♕g4 ♘e7 28.h4 ♕g6 29.hg5
♘f6 30.gf6 ♕g4 31.fe7

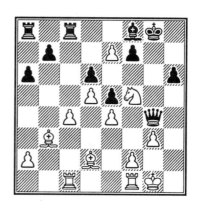

31...♗g7 32.c5 dc5 33.f3 ♕g6
34.d6 ♔h7 35.♔g2 h5 36.♖h1 ♗f6
37.g4 ♖g8 38.♔f1 b5 39.♗d5, 1-0

Game 240
Tal,M—N.N.
Stuttgart 1958

1.e4 c5 2.♘f3 d6 3.d4 cd4 4.♘d4
♘f6 5.♘c3 g6 6.♗e3 ♗g7 7.f3 ♘c6
8.♕d2 ♗d7 9.0-0-0 ♕a5 10.♔b1
♖c8 11.g4 h6 12.h4 a6 13.♗e2 ♘e5
14.g5 hg5 15.hg5 ♖h1 16.gf6 ♖d1
17.♘d1 ♕d2 18.fg7, 1-0

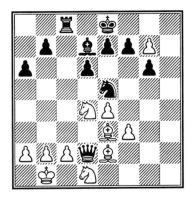

final position

Game 241
Larsen,B—Spassky,B
Belgrade 1970

1.b3 e5 2.♗b2 ♘c6 3.c4 ♘f6 4.♘f3
e4 5.♘d4 ♗c5 6.♘c6 dc6 7.e3 ♗f5
8.♕c2 ♕e7 9.♗e2 0-0-0 10.f4 ♘g4
11.g3 h5 12.h3 h4 13.hg4 hg3
14.♖g1 ♖h1 15.♖h1 g2 16.♖f1 ♕h4
17.♔d1 gf1=♕, 0-1 (Excelsior!)

(see next diagram)

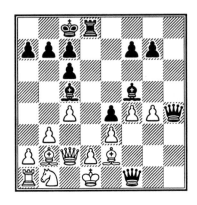

final position

Game 242
Uhlmann,W—Kovacevic,V
Rovinj-Zagreb 1971

1.d4 d5 2.c4 e6 3.♘c3 ♗b4 4.♘f3
♘f6 5.♕a4 ♘c6 6.♗g5 h6 7.cd5
ed5 8.♗h4 g5 9.♗g3 ♘e4 10.♖c1
h5 11.♘e5 ♗d7 12.♕b3 ♕e7
13.♕d5 h4 14.♕e4 hg3 15.♘d7
♖h2 16.♖h2 gh2

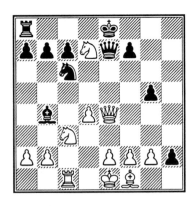

17.♕h7 0-0-0 18.♕h2 ♖d7 19.♕h8
♖d8 20.♕h3 ♔b8 21.a3 ♗a5 22.d5
♘e5 23.e4 g4 24.♕h5 f5 25.♕f5

♖f8 26.♕e6 ♕g5 27.♔d1 a6
28.♖c2 ♗b6 29.d6 ♖d8 30.♖d2 cd6
31.♘d5 ♗c5 32.b4 ♗a7 33.♕e7
♕g8 34.♖c2 ♖d7 35.♕h4 ♖f7
36.♕g3 ♕f8 37.♔e1 ♗d4 38.♘e3
♖f4 39.♘d5 ♖e4 40.♖e2 ♗f2, 0-1

Game 243
Lobigas,J—Micheli
Skopje 1972

1.e4 c5 2.♘f3 d6 3.d4 cd4 4.♘d4
♘f6 5.♘c3 a6 6.♗g5 e6 7.f4 ♗e7
8.♕f3 ♕c7 9.0-0-0 ♘bd7 10.g4 b5
11.♗f6 ♘f6 12.g5 ♘d7 13.a3 ♖b8
14.h4 b4 15.ab4 ♖b4 16.h5 ♕b6
17.♘b3 ♗b7 18.g6 0-0 19.h6 fg6
20.hg7

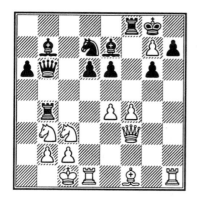

20...♖f6 21.♕h3 h5 22.♗d3 ♘c5
23.♘c5 ♕c5 24.♖hg1 ♗c8 25.e5
♖ff4 26.♕h5, 1-0

Game 244
Chiburdanidze,M—Ubilava,E
Tbilisi 1976

1.e4 ♘f6 2.e5 ♘d5 3.d4 d6 4.♘f3
♗g4 5.♗e2 e6 6.h3 ♗h5 7.0-0 ♗e7

8.c4 ♘b6 9.♘c3 0-0 10.♗e3 ♘8d7
11.b3 de5 12.♘e5 ♗e2 13.♕e2 c6
14.♖fd1 ♘f6 15.♗f4 ♖e8 16.♕f3 a5
17.♖ac1 h6 18.♖d3 ♗f8 19.♗e3 a4
20.♘e4 ♘bd7 21.♖cd1 ♕a5
22.♘f6 ♘f6 23.♗h6 ab3 24.ab3
♕b4 25.♗g5 ♗e7 26.h4 ♕d6 27.h5
c5 28.h6 cd4 29.h7, 1-0

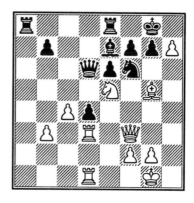

final position

Game 245
Kasparov,G—Vaganian,R
Novgorod 1995

1.d4 e6 2.c4 d5 3.♘c3 ♗e7 4.♘f3
♘f6 5.♗f4 0-0 6.e3 c5 7.dc5 ♗c5
8.♕c2 ♘c6 9.a3 ♕a5 10.0-0-0 ♗e7
11.h4 dc4 12.♗c4 b6 13.♘g5 ♗a6
14.♘ce4 g6 15.♘f6 ♗f6 16.♘e4
♗e7 17.♗a6 ♕a6 18.♔b1 ♕b7
19.h5 ♖ac8 20.hg6 ♘b4 21.gh7

(see next diagram)

21...♔h8 22.♗e5 f6 23.♘f6 ♗f6
24.♗f6, 1-0

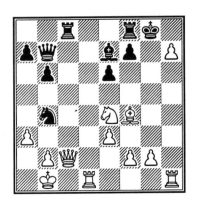

After 21.gh7

20...♗f3 21.♗f6 ♗h1 22.g5 ♘e4
23.♘e4 ♗e4 24.♘g4 h5 25.gh6 b3
26.♕a5 ♖a5 27.♗d8, 1-0

Game 246
Atalik,S—Cela,A
Chalkida 1996

1.d4 ♘f6 2.c4 g6 3.♘c3 ♗g7 4.e4
d6 5.♗e2 0-0 6.♗g5 ♘bd7 7.f3
c6 8.♘h3 e5 9.d5 cd5 10.cd5 ♘c5
11.♘f2 a5 12.♕d2 ♗d7 13.g4 a4
14.h4 ♕a5 15.h5 ♖fc8 16.♖b1 b5
17.♘cd1 b4 18.♘e3 ♗b5 19.h6
♗e2 20.hg7

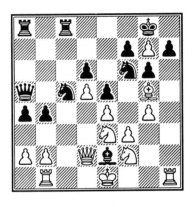

Part Four

The Mutual Steeplechase

Game 247
Spielmann,R—Nimzowitsch,A
Bled 1931

1.e4 c6 2.♘f3 d5 3.♘c3 de4 4.♘e4 ♘f6 5.♘g3 c5 6.♗c4 a6 7.a4 ♘c6 8.d3 g6 9.♗e3 ♗g7 10.0-0 b6 11.c3 0-0 12.h3 ♗b7 13.♕e2 ♘a5 14.♗a2 ♗d5 15.♘d2 ♗a2 16.♖a2 ♘d5 17.♘c4 ♘c6 18.a5 b5 19.♘b6 ♘b6 20.ab6 ♕b6 21.♘e4 ♕c7 22.♘c5 a5 23.d4 ♖fb8 24.f4 e6 25.♖aa1 ♘e7 26.g4 ♘d5 27.♖f3 a4 28.♗d2 ♕c6 29.♘e4 b4 30.f5 ef5 31.gf5 a3 32.ba3 bc3 33.f6 cd2 34.fg7

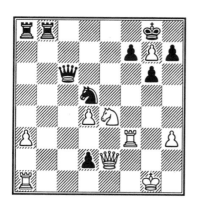

34...♖e8 35.♕d3 ♖e4 36.♕e4 ♖e8 37.♕h4 ♘c3 38.♖ff1 ♕d5, 0-1

Game 248
Guimard,C—Rossetto,H
Mar del Plata

1.d4 ♘f6 2.♘f3 g6 3.♗g5 ♗g7 4.♘bd2 d5 5.e3 0-0 6.♗d3 c5 7.c3 ♕b6 8.♖b1 ♘c6 9.0-0 e5 10.♗f6 ♗f6 11.e4 ♗e6 12.ed5 ♗d5 13.♗e4 ♖fd8 14.♗d5 ♖d5 15.♘e4 ♗e7 16.c4 ♖dd8 17.d5 f5 18.♘ed2 e4 19.dc6 ef3 20.♕e1 ♗f6 21.cb7 fg2 22.ba8=♕ gf1=♕

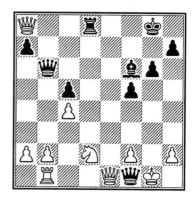

23.♘f1 ♖a8 24.♘e3 ♖e8 25.♕d1 ♗d4 26.♘d5 ♕d8 27.♕f3 ♕h4 28.b3 ♖e4 29.h3 ♔g7 30.♔f1 ♗f2 31.♔g2 ♗d4 32.♖f1 ♕g5 33.♔h1 ♕d2 34.♘f4 ♖e1 35.♘h5 ♔h6 36.♘g3 ♖f1 37.♘f1 ♕f2 38.♕f2 ♗f2 39.♔g2 ♗d4 40.♘g3 ♔g5 41.♘e2 ♗e5 42.♘c1 ♔f6 43.♘d3 ♗d6, 0-1

Game 249
Plaskett,J—Watson,W
Brighton 983

1.e4 c5 2.♘f3 d6 3.d4 cd4 4.♘d4
♘f6 5.♘c3 g6 6.♗e3 ♗g7 7.f3 0-0
8.♕d2 ♘c6 9.g4 ♗e6 10.0-0-0 ♘d4
11.♗d4 ♕a5 12.a3 ♖fc8 13.h4
♖ab8 14.h5 b5 15.h6 b4 16.hg7 ba3
17.♕h6 ab2

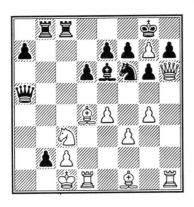

18.♔d2 ♗g4 19.♗f6 ♗h5 20.♗d4
e5 21.♖h5 gh5 22.♕g5 ♕b4
23.♗d3 ♕d4 24.♘d5 ♕f2 25.♗e2
♖c2 26.♔c2 ♕e2 27.♔c3 ♕f3
28.♔c4 ♕b3#, 0-1

Excelsior in Chess Compositions

There in the twilight cold and gray,
Lifeless, but beautiful, he lay,
And from the sky, serene and far,
A voice fell, like a falling star,
Excelsior!
H.Longfellow, "Excelsior"

The term Excelsior was the motto of
a famous puzzle created by Sam Loyd
in 1858, at the Paul Morphy chess
club in New York.

Game 250
Loyd,S
Era 1861

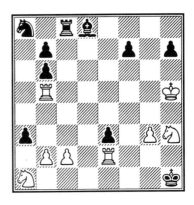

Mate in Five

1.b4 ♖c5 2.bc5 a2 3.c6 (△ 4.♖d5)
3...♗c7 4.cb7 ♗g3 5.ba8=♕#

Sam Loyd has expressed, in orginal
fashion, the connection between poetry on the chess board and poetry in
literature. Like Longfellow's hero,
the pawn attains lofty peaks of performance under the bannered
motto, "Higher and higher!"

The idea behind the problem – to
perform a pawn march from its initial
position to the 8th rank and promotion – was already known at this
time. Loyd's creation, however, stim-
ulated in chess circles a general in-

terest in the subject. Later the theme
was taken up by several chess com-
posers; below are some examples of
their creative work.

Game 251
Labourdonnais

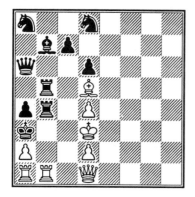

Mate in Seven

1.♕b3 ♖b3 2.ab3 ♚b4 3.ba4 ♚a5
4.ab5 ♚b6 5.ba6 ♚a7 6.ab7 ♚b8
7.ba8=♕ #

Game 252
Meier,H
Strategie 1882

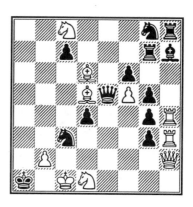

Mate in Seven

1.bc3 gh2 2.cd4 gh3 3.de5 gh4 4.ef6
cd6 5.fg7 ♘f6 6.gh8=♕ h1=♕ 7.♕f6#

Game 253
Meier,H
Deutsches Wochenschach 1885

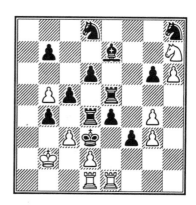

Mate in Seven

1.♚b3 e3 2.de3 ♚e4 3.ed4 ♚d5
4.de5 ♚e6 5.ed6 ♚d7 6.de7 ♚e8
7.ed8=♘ #

Game 254
Kubbel,L
Deutsches Wochenschach 1910

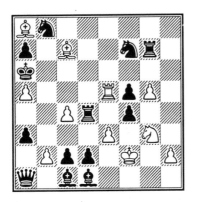

Mate in Seven

1.b4 fg3 2.hg3 ♖f4 3.gf4 ♕e5 4.fe5
♘d6 5.ed6 ♖c7 6.dc7 ♗f3
7.cb8=♘#

Game 255
Kubbel,L
Shakhmaty v SSSR 1939

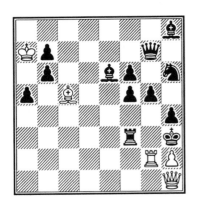

Mate in Seven

1.♖g1! (△ 2.♕g2#) **1...♖g3**
(1...♖f2 2.♗f2 ♗d5 3.♕d5 ♔h2

4.♕g2#) **2.hg3 ♔g4 3.gh4 ♔h5**
(3...♔f4 4.♗d6 ♔e3 5.♖g3 ♔d4
6.♕d1 ♔c4 7.♕d3#) **4.hg5 ♔g6**
5.gh6 ♔h7 (5...♔f7 6.♕h5 ♔g8
7.h7#) **6.hg7 ♔g8 7.gh8=♘#**

Game 256
Troitzky,A
Eskilstuna Kuriren 1916

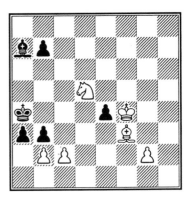

White to play and win

1.♗d1! ♗b8 2.♔e4 a2 3.cb3 ♔a5
4.b4 ♔a6 5.b5 ♔a7 (5...♔b5 6.♘c3
+−) 6.b6 ♔a8 7.♘c7 ♗c7 8.bc7
a1=♕ 9.c8=♕ ♔a7 10.♕c5 ♔b8
11.♕d6 ♔a7 12.♕a3 +−

Game 257
Rinck, H
Bachler Nachrichten 1937

White to play and win

1.♔d5 ♗e5 2.g3 ♔f5 3.g4 ♔f6
4.g5 ♔f5 5.g6 ♔f6 6.g7 +−

Game 258
Giorgiev, G
1938

White to play and draw

1.♔b5 ♔d5 2.c4 ♔d6 3.c5 ♔d7
4.c6 ♔d6 5.c7 ♖h8 6.♔a6 ♔d7

7.♔a7 ♔c6 8.c8=♕ ♖c8 9.b7 ♖c7
10.♔a8 ♖b7 =

Game 259
Korolkov, V
64-Shakhmatnoje Obozrenie
1969

White to play and win

1.bc3 ♔c5 2.cd4 ♔d6 3.de5 ♔e7
4.ef6 ♔f8 5.fg7 ♔g8 6.gh8=♕ ♔h8
7.♕b2 ♔g8 8.♕e2 +−

March of the
Doubled Pawns

We conclude with a curious trio.

Game 260
Tylkowski—Wojciechowski
Poznan 1931

1.f4 d5 2.e3 c5 3.♘f3 ♘c6 4.♗b5
♗g4 5.0-0 e6 6.d3 ♗e7 7.♘c3 d4
8.♘b1 ♘f6 9.e4 0-0 10.♗c6 bc6

11.c3 dc3 12.♘c3 ♗f3 13.♖f3 ♘g4
14.♔h1 ♕d4 15.♕g1 ♕g1 16.♔g1
♗d8 17.♗e3 ♘e3 18.♖e3 ♗b6
19.♖d1 h6 20.e5 f6 21.ef6 ♖f6
22.♖f3 c4 23.d4 c5 24.d5 ed5
25.♖d5 ♔h7 26.♖d7 ♖d8 27.♖b7
♖g6 28.♖g3 ♖g3 29.hg3 ♖d2
30.♘a4 ♖b2 31.♘b2

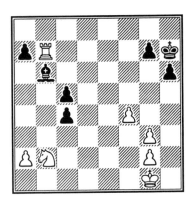

31...c3! 32.♖b6 c4! 33.♖b4 a5!
34.♘c4 c2! 35.♘a5 c1=♕ 36.♔h2
♕c5 37.♖b2 ♕a5 38.g4 ♕e1 39.g3
h5 40.gh5 ♔h6 (...), 1-0

The same idea is seen in the following game, given with commentary
by the 3rd world champion, J.R.
Capablanca.

Game 261
Ortueta—Sanz
Madrid 1933

1.e4 e6 2.d3 (Not as new as one
might think. Back in 1911
Nimzowitsch was playing this move,
and, if I am not mistaken, he used it
against me in the 1911 San Sebastian
Tournament) **2...d5 3.♘c3** (Here
Nimzowitsch would play 3.♘d2 with
the aim of bringing about a position
with White which is like the
Hanham Variation of the Philidor
Defense. Nimzowitsch's idea contains a general plan, but here White
soon plays d3-d4 which, so to speak,
condemns his complete opening,
since it merely involves the loss of
tempo) **3...♘f6** (He could also play
3...c5 with an excellent position)
4.e5 ♘fd7 5.f4 ♗b4 (Of very
doubtful value, since it gives White
the opportunity to play 6.a3) **6.♗d2**
(An overly defensive move, which
gives the initiative to Black without
compensation of any kind; this is sufficient to refute entirely White's plan
of development) **6...0-0 7.♘f3 f6
8.d4 c5 9.♘b5** (White wastes the
best opportunity offered by the bad
position of Black's Bishop at b4, the
result of his opponent's weak fifth
move. The text move leads to a very
inferior game, if not completely lost.
Here it is necessary to play 9.a3! cd4
[9...♗a5 10.b4! cb4 11.ab4 ♗b4
12.♘b5 ♗d2 13.♕d2] 10.ab4 dc3
11.♗c3, and in return for a pawn
White has a formidable position)
9...fe5 (A serious error which
should have cost Black the full bene-
fit of White's ninth move. The correct line would have been 9...♗d2
10.♕d2 cd4 11.♘bd4 ♘c5) **10.de5**
(Another mistake. 10.♗b4 was the
right move, and if 10...cb4 11.fe5

Part Four 115

with a good position) **10...♖f4? 11.c3 ♖e4 12.♗e2 ♗a5 13.0-0** (The situation has completely changed owing to Black's insistence on incorrect complications. Although he has won a pawn his pieces are undeveloped, making it almost impossible for him to defend himself. Such things can sometimes happen in closed positions, but not in open positions like the present one. Black's only positional compensation is the strong central situation of his pawns and, above all, the fact that White's Bishops are not aggressively posted) **13...♘e5** (This move seems inadequate and is not all in accordance with the previous note. It is truly strange to see enthusiasts violate so frequently the fundamental principles of chess. The situation after White's 13th move is certainly difficult, but following the idea in the previous note, the only move was 13...c4 to prevent the entry of White's Bishop at d3. If then 14.♘d6, there follows 14...♖e5 15.♘c8 ♕c8 16.♘e5 ♘e5 with good drawing chances) **14.♘e5 ♖e5 15.♗f4 ♖f5 16.♗d3** (Now the White Bishops come into play, and Black is saved only by the lack of energy with which White carries out the attack) **16...♖f6** (Black is two miserable pawns ahead, but the whole of his Queenside is still at home, while his Bishop at a5 is not doing anything. White, on the other hand, can quickly bring all his pieces to the attack) **17.♕c2** (This move is a disaster. White limits, and almost ruins, the scope of action of his best piece. With 17.♕h5 h6 18.♗h6 gh6 [If 18...♖h6 19.♕f7 and mate in two] 19.♖f6 ♕f6 20.♖f1 and there is no defense. After 17.♕h5 Black could play 17...g6!, but after 18.♕h4 there is no defense against the threat of 19.♗g5. For example, 18...c4 19.♗g5 ♖f1 20.♖f1 ♕b6 21.♔h1 cd3 22.♖f7 ♔f7 [If 22...h5 then 23.♕f4 ♘d7 24.♖e7] 23.♕h7 ♔f8 24.♕e7 ♔g8 25.♗f6) **17...h6 18.♗e5 ♘d7 19.♗f6 ♘f6 20.♖f6 ♕f6 21.♖f1 ♕e7 22.♗h7 ♔h8 23.♕g6 ♗d7 24.♖f7 ♕g5 25.♕g5 hg5 26.♖d7 ♔h7 27.♖b7 ♗b6** (A weak move which makes a relatively easy ending difficult. The right move was 27...c4) **28.c4** (With this move White is practically assured of a draw. If there is any way for Black to win it is extremely difficult, and in my opinion, it is impossible) **24...dc4 29.♘c3** (29.♘d6 was the right move, and one cannot see how Black could win. With the text move White misses his last chance of drawing) **29...♖d8 30.h3 ♖d2 31.♘a4 ♖b2** (A most brilliant ending, although it seems that Black could also win without having to avail himself of such resources) **32.♘b2**

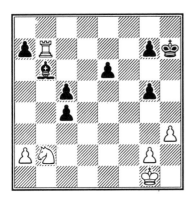

32...c3 33.罝b6 c4 34.罝b4 a5
(The finishing touch to this short but pretty combination) **35.公c4 c2** (It is not necessary to give the three or four further moves that were played before White resigned. The ending of this game, moves 31-34, is an extremely beautiful miniature. It is a pity that the rest of the game is not at the same level as such a sublime ending), **0-1** (J.R. Capablanca. *El Ajedrez Espause*, Feb. 1936, pp. 39-41)

Game 262
Bejnfest,B
Shakhmaty v SSSR 1976

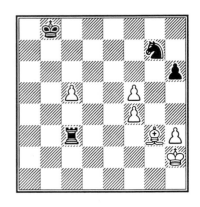

White to play and win

1.f6 罝g3 2.f5 罝g2 3.堂h1 罝g5
4.h4 罝h5 5.堂g1 罝h4 6.f7 罝g4
7.堂h2 罝h4 8.堂g2 +−

Postscript

Our next issue of *The Tactician's Handbook* will be dedicated to the fascinating world of "Domination," the trapping and containment of various pieces. One well known example is the first game of the world championship match between Fischer and Spassky.

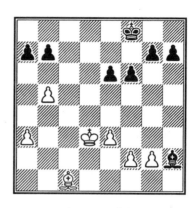

After 29...♗h2

Game 263
Spassky,B—Fischer,R
Reykjavik 1972

1.d4 ♘f6 2.c4 e6 3.♘f3 d5 4.♘c3 ♗b4 5.e3 0-0 6.♗d3 c5 7.0-0 ♘c6 8.a3 ♗a5 9.♘e2 dc4 10.♗c4 ♗b6 11.dc5 ♕d1 12.♖d1 ♗c5 13.b4 ♗e7 14.♗b2 ♗d7 15.♖ac1 ♖fd8 16.♘ed4 ♘d4 17.♘d4 ♗a4 18.♗b3 ♗b3 19.♘b3 ♖d1 20.♖d1 ♖c8 21.♔f1 ♔f8 22.♔e2 ♘e4 23.♖c1 ♖c1 24.♗c1 f6 25.♘a5 ♘d6 26.♔d3 ♗d8 27.♘c4 ♗c7 28.♘d6 ♗d6 29.b5 ♗h2

(see next diagram)

30.g3! (Quite a typical Domination. White catches the opponent's Bishop "behind the lines") **30...h5 31.♔e2 h4 32.♔f3 ♔e7** (Useless is 32...h3 33.♔g4 ♗g1 34.♔h3 ♗f2 35.♗d2!, and the Bishop is still trapped) **33.♔g2 hg3 34.fg3 ♗g3 35.♔g3** (White has an extra piece, and gains the victory after further errors) **35...♔d6 36.a4 ♔d5 37.♗a3 ♔e4 38.♗c5 a6 39.b6 f5 40.♔h4 f4?** (40...♔d5! 41.♗d4 [41.♗e7 ♔e4 42.♗g5 e5, △ 43...f4] 41...e5 42.♗c3 ♔e4 43.♔g5 f4 44.ef4 ef4 ±, △ ...♔d5-c4. S. Gligoric) **41.ef4 ♔f4 42.♔h5 ♔f5 43.♗e3 ♔e4 44.♗f2 ♔f5 45.♗h4 e5 46.♗g5 e4 47.♗e3 ♔f6 48.♔g4 ♔e5 49.♔g5 ♔d5 50.♔f5 a5 51.♗f2 g5 52.♔g5 ♔c4 53.♔f5 ♔b4 54.♔e4 ♔a4 55.♔d5 ♔b5 56.♔d6, 1-0**

Index of Players

Note: the numbers refer to game numbers.

About the Author

Victor Charushin was born in the Russian Republic of Udmurtija in 1932. He is by profession a civil engineer, lecturing at the Academy of Architecture and Building in Nizhny Novgorod where he lives – but his first love is chess. Victor is well known in the world of correspondence chess, and has placed among the prize-winners in several European Championships. In 1986 Victor earned the ICCF International Master title, after which his attention turned to writing. Charushin is the author of over twenty books, including biographies of Alekhine and Bogoljubow.

The Tactician's Handbook

This series offers a radical new understanding of chess combinations. Each volume explores in depth a single and fundamental element of tactical play. Bringing together hundreds of carefully chosen examples, and presented in ICCF IM Charushin's unique style, The Tactician's Handbook systematically prepares the reader for real-world chess combat. Together, the series amounts to a combinational boot camp, a battle plan for tactical victory, and a storm on the summit of mastery in chess. Are you ready?

Vol. 1 — Alekhine's Block

Vol. 2 — Combination Cross

Vol. 3 — Mitrofanov's Deflection

Vol. 4 — Lasker's Combination

Vol. 5 — The Steeplechase

Vol. 6 — Domination (available 2000)

Vol. 7 — Rare Combinations (available 2000)